GRO
EXOTIC PLANTS
indoors

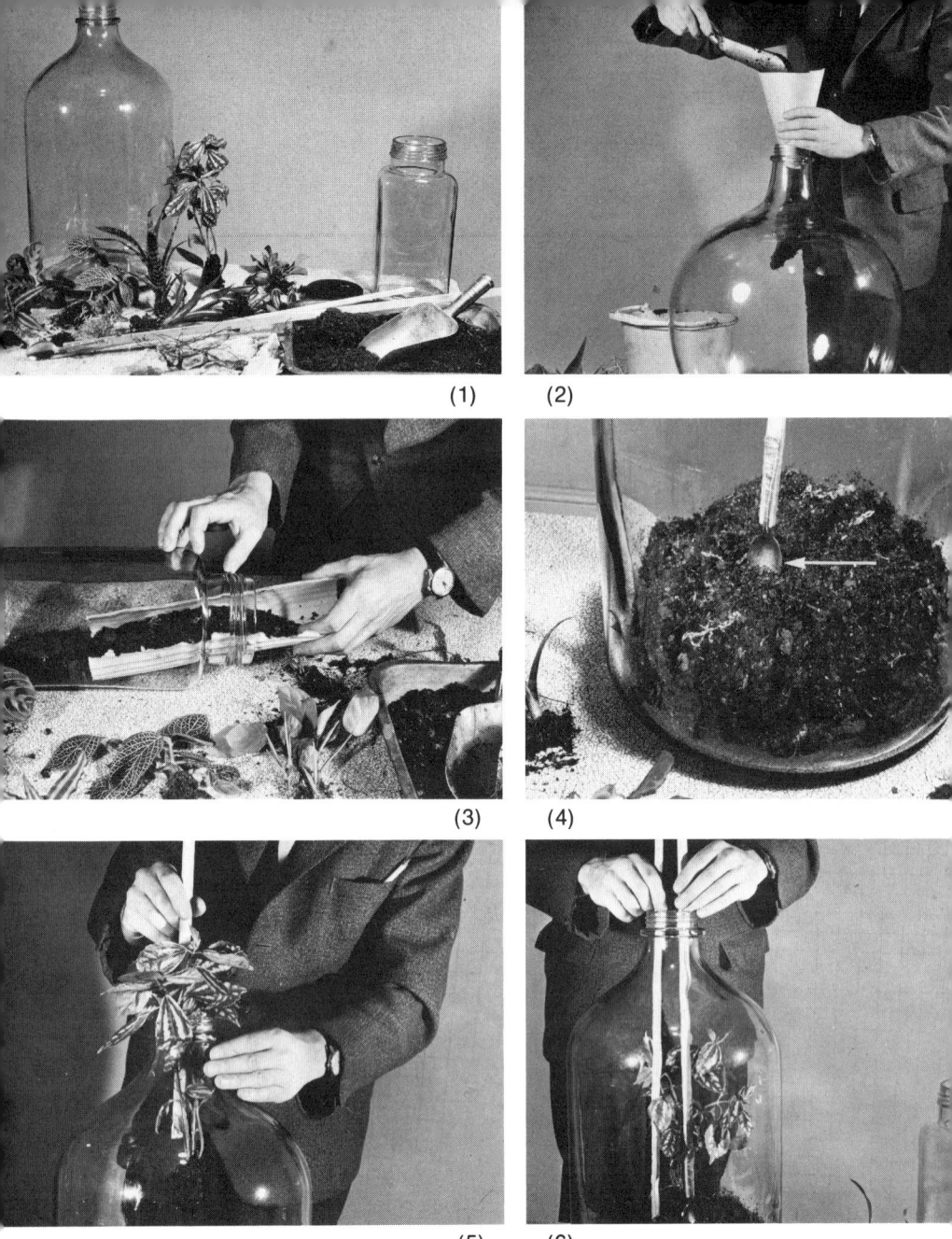

MAKING A BOTTLE GARDEN

(1) Materials and plants ready for making a bottle garden. (2) A cardboard funnel keeps the soil from dirtying the sides of the bottle. (3) A cardboard guide is used to introduce soil into the jar. (4) Holes for the plants are made with a spoon tied to the end of a stick. (5) A plant is lowered into the bottle by means of a bent wire fastened to a stick and inserted into the root ball of the plant. (6) The final position of the plant is adjusted by manipulating two sticks.

Growing Exotic Plants Indoors

R.H. Menage

Henry Regnery Company · Chicago

Library of Congress Cataloging in Publication Data
Menage, Ronald Herbert.
    Growing exotic plants indoors.

    Includes indexes.
    1. House plants.   I. Title.
SB419.M53   635.9'65   74-30266
ISBN 0-8092-8874-5
ISBN 0-8092-8248-8 pbk.

Special Horticultural Consultant
John A. Lundgren, B.S.
Chief Horticulturalist (retired), Chicago Park District

Copyright © 1966, 1975 by R. H. Menage
All rights reserved
Published by Henry Regnery Company
180 North Michigan Avenue, Chicago, Illinois 60601
Manufactured in the United States of America
Library of Congress Catalog Card Number: 74-30266
International Standard Book Number: 0-8092-8874-5 (cloth)
                                     0-8092-8248-8 (paper)

CONTENTS

ACKNOWLEDGMENTS   vii

INTRODUCTION   ix

1 KEEPING PLANTS HEALTHY INDOORS   1

Treatment of indoor plants—Plants in pots and planters—Plant cases—Plant windows—The conservatory and sun porch—Palms—Culture of palms—Bottle gardens—House plants from seed

2 BONSAI   39

Characteristics of Bonsai—Growing Bonsai—Displaying Bonsai

3 TOUCH-SENSITIVE, MOTILE, AND CARNIVOROUS PLANTS   47

Movement in plants—Touch-sensitive and motile plants for pots—Other sensitive plants—The nature of carnivorous or insectivorous plants—Culture of carnivorous plants—The Cephalotaceae—The Droseraceae—The Lentibulariaceae—The Nepenthaceae—The Sarraceniaceae—Experimenting with carnivorous plants

4 STRANGE OR UNUSUAL PLANTS 79

Aristolochia—Bromeliads (the pineapple family)—Calonyction (Moonflower)—Clianthus (Glory Pea)—*Davallia mariesii* (Japanese Fern Balls)— *Lophophora williamsii* (Mescal Button)—Musa (Banana)—Platycerium (Staghorn fern)—Sauromatum (Monarch of the East)—Strelitzia (Bird of Paradise flower)

5 GROWING PLANTS FROM SEED 105

Viability, storage, germination—Essential germination requirements—Practical sowing and germinating techniques: Soil mixes for germination, germination without soil, seed dressings, incubators and propagators, containers for germination—Sowing the seed—After-care of seedlings: soil mixes and fertilizers for seedlings and potted plants, germinating fern spores—Cultural troubles with uncommon plants

SUPPLIERS OF UNUSUAL AND EXOTIC PLANTS 128

GENERAL INDEX 130

BOTANICAL INDEX 135

ACKNOWLEDGMENTS

DURING the several years that it has taken to plan this book and grow the plants for photographing and drawing, I have received numerous gifts of plants and seeds. I am especially indebted to the cooperation and friendly help of Charles W.J. Unwin, F.L.S., who has provided me with much plant material.

I am also grateful for the help given by Alan Roger, who gave valuable advice incorporated in the section on Bonsai, allowed me to photograph in his Kensington garden, and supplied me with photographs of his extensive Bonsai garden in Scotland—one of the largest in the British Isles—on which I based the very simplified drawing on page 46.

Plate 1 was kindly given by Indoor Gardening Ltd, and Plate 3 by Medway Buildings Ltd. Plate 2 is a photocopy that I made of an illustration that was originally printed in Vol. 1 of *The Garden* in 1872.

INTRODUCTION

THE vegetable kingdom is so vast that, however industrious the gardener, only a comparatively insignificant number of plant species can be grown in a lifetime. Such tremendous scope can make horticulture a rich source of never-ending interest and wonder, but few people seem to take advantage of this variety. The average gardener is content to grow the same plants year after year. There is no doubt about it: the spirit of adventure is markedly lacking—or we would see many more different plants among the standard garden and greenhouse displays. Even city parks and gardens seem to be remarkably unenterprising.

Perhaps one reason for this apathy is the little to be found in gardening literature to relate the often intriguing history of plants or reveal their sometimes astonishing uses. Another reason may be that too frequently, when a particularly interesting plant is described, one is left without an idea of where to obtain it. This book is an attempt to rectify these two possible deficiencies and at the same time to show how much more fascinating it can be to grow plants if one knows more about them.

x   Introduction

It is said that to engage the concentration of the public a subject must involve religion, crime, and sex, and that these may be thought to have little to do with gardening. Yet if it is pointed out that a certain cactus has been used as "bread" in communion service because it produces colorful hallucinations, that a particular herb is the source of a fatal poison, that an extract of an attractive flower is a powerful aphrodisiac—perhaps then it is possible to claim attentive readers.

In this book I hope to arouse interest by analogous tactics, although I have had to apply a certain amount of discretion so as not to provoke the fury of the Church or the attention of the Law. I am mainly concerned, in fact, with introducing a number of plants that have unusual qualities—a strange romantic atmosphere about them—as well as being decorative, useful, or instructive.

Some of the plants are little known; others are familiar to many gardeners but nevertheless have features that are surprising. All the plants described can readily be grown in the United States, in many cases indoors, and in all cases sufficient cultural information is included.

In all cases, too, I have either grown the plants myself or been concerned in their uses or economic applications. Most of the illustrations are of my own plants, and to give some idea of their natural size I have superimposed a one-inch scale or included a familiar object in the photographs.

Although there are a few exceptions, described because of their outstanding fascination, the majority of the plants are easily obtainable: I have deliberately limited my selection to those that are.

Gardening can be an adventure. The plants described in this book should be adequate proof of this statement.

growing exotic plants indoors

1

KEEPING PLANTS HEALTHY INDOORS

MAN seems to have a natural instinct to grow plants. Primitive man was very much more plant-conscious than we are nowadays because the acquisition of food depended on his own initiative; today it is easily possible for the majority of our population to live out their lives without even seeing anything grow or having to worry about the origin of food. However, given a little encouragement, the spark of the "close to nature" instinct can be fanned into flame, especially in the many people who, through living in large cities, are starved of the placid and soothing atmosphere created by foliage and flowers.

As apartment buildings proliferate, so the desire of their inmates to bring greenery into their homes grows. It is also indicative of the deficiencies of much modern architecture that plants are being used more and more to soften harsh lines. A well-planned blending of concrete, plastic, glass, glistening metal, and suitable vegetation can have a most pleasing and relaxing effect, but whisk away the plants and the modern building becomes a home for machines and robots—not for human beings!

Unfortunately, apart from the aspidistra, there are few plants that can be termed "hardy" indoor plants, and even the aspidistra will not look its best if it is seriously neglected. Many of the newly introduced house plants are of tropical or subtropical origin and need considerable attention. To many people the newer house plants are strange and unfamiliar, but this does not mean that they are any more difficult to grow than native plants brought into the house; in fact, most of them are a good deal easier to grow.

The "modern" house plant earns its title because it is more suited to the modern style of home construction, in which a uniform temperature, exclusion of drafts, and a reasonable amount of diffused light are important features. Few of the modern house plants will survive for long—particularly in winter—in an environment where the temperature is subject to enormous fluctuations. Plants used to brighten the office or place of business may suffer from the misfortune of being left to freeze or go dry over the weekend. The number of failures due to such circumstances can be reduced by careful selection of plants or by providing more suitable growing conditions, but it must be realized that the selection of plants that withstand a certain amount of neglect and fluctuation in temperature is not very great, and it is better to try to improve conditions for the plants. (A simple way to keep a plant moist and healthy if it has to be left without attention for a few days is to cover it, pot and all, with a plastic bag.)

The Victorians knew what they were about when they grew the aspidistra, and it is still one of the best foliage plants for the house. If it is displayed with a group of other foliage plants in a suitable container and the leaves are kept clean, it can look most attractive. The ivies are also among the few plants resistant to some neglect. *Hedera canariensis* is one of the most colorful, with deep green, pale green, and cream colored leaves. This ivy can be acclimatized to grow in quite cold rooms and will put up with some wide temperature changes. Other plants resistant to cold—but not freezing—are *Fatsia japonica,* fatshederas, the spiky-leaved chlorophytums, *Stenocarpus sinuatus,* the Christmas-tree-like *Araucaria excelsa,* and many cacti and other succulents.

Few plants will survive in an atmosphere near open gas burners. Coal gas and its products of combustion are poisonous to vegetation. However, rooms fitted with modern gas burners can usually accommodate plants, because if the flame is adjusted properly and the flue is effective, no fumes or gas should ever escape into the room.

All plants must have some light, but their needs vary considerably and they can be selected according to the amount of light available. Philodendrons, some ferns, some palms, marantas, *Zebrina pendula,* peperomias, and *Begonia rex* are a few plants that prefer shade. Although plenty of light is an advantage for many house plants, direct sunlight can be harmful, and a plant indoors on a sunny windowsill can quickly shrivel. A window or aspect facing north is probably the best situation for the majority of house plants.

Watering, humidity, and temperature are the main difficulties in growing house plants successfully, and it is to the solving of these problems that the main part of this chapter is devoted.

Plants in Pots and Planters

Since plants require a moist atmosphere and a moist but not waterlogged soil, it follows that the type of container given to a house plant largely governs whether it will grow successfully. The Victorians were very fond of the "art pot"—an often highly ornamented and colored large bowl-shaped glazed pot in which the clay pot stood. If a little water was put in the bottom of the art pot and the clay pot was raised just above the surface, the soil of the plant kept moist for a long time because evaporation from the clay pot was greatly reduced. In addition, water vapor rising from the art pot helped to maintain a local moist atmosphere around the plant.

The same sort of technique can be used today, choosing

glazed or plastic pots to suit the decor of the room.

Growing the plant in a plastic flowerpot greatly helps to keep a nicely moist soil. A plastic pot requires less water than a clay pot, but as far as house plants are concerned this is a distinct advantage. Clay pots are still best for subjects that prefer a rather dry soil and for epiphytic plants that need a well-aerated soil.

It is often claimed that plastic containers keep the soil warmer than do clay pots, but there is no truth to this. The soil in any type of nonporous container may be at a very slightly higher temperature than that in a porous clay pot. The reason for this is that evaporation of water from the porous surface causes a lowering in temperature, just as in the case of evaporative coolers, which work on a similar principle. In practice, the temperature of the soil in clay or plastic pots is much the same, and any difference is unlikely to influence growth.

Fiberglass containers are similar in nature to plastic pots, but usually they are more expensive. They are also resistant to weather and can be used out of doors as window boxes or terrace pots.

If one does not want plastic, real stone and marble containers are also available at high prices. For some purposes teak planters and tubs may blend better with the surrounding architecture, but, again, these are expensive. Somewhat cheaper are cedar or redwood containers, treated with a preservative to prevent them from rotting.

For most indoor plants the plastic container will be found the most suitable, but it is essential to remember that these, when purchased, may have no drainage holes. If weakened areas are provided on the base, these should be pressed out to afford drainage if the plants are to be grown directly in the pot or planter.

The correct way to use ornamental containers of any material indoors is to fill them with moist peat. The pots in which the plants are growing are then buried in the peat so

Keeping Plants Healthy Indoors   5

that their rims are just covered. This method solves some of the difficulties associated with growing house plants:

1. It provides an attractive finish, because the plants look better against the dark peat, and the pots are hidden.
2. It keeps the soil in the pots moist for a long time.
3. It maintains a local moist atmosphere for the plants.
4. It takes up any excess water when the plants are watered and hence prevents waterlogging of the soil.

Any pot or planter without a drainage hole should be prepared as follows: a quarter of the pot should be filled with a reservoir of gravel (not limestone) or potsherds (pieces of broken clay flower pot). This reservoir will act as a French drain to collect the excess water that runs through the soil. Then use good-quality soil to fill the remainder of the pot, leaving a small space at the top. The tricky part of being successful involves determining exactly how much water to give the plant and how frequently. It is very unlikely that you will be able to predict proper watering frequency, because drying out depends on the usual factors controlling transpiration: humidity, temperature, size of plant in relation to container, how long it has been growing in container, etc.

There fortunately is a method of determining frequency of watering that works in almost all cases. Examine the plant every day (or at least until a frequency system has been established). If it is dry, water it; if it is not dry, *don't* water it. If too much water has been given and there is still some standing on the surface after ten to fifteen minutes, pour off the excess and next time do not give it so much.

Actually, the space left in the top of a container should hold the proper amount of water to soak the pot to the bottom plus some excess for run through. The correct space is more or less standard for standard containers: 1/4 inch for a 2-1/2-inch pot, 1/2 inch for a 4-inch pot, 3/4 inch for a 6-inch pot, and 1 inch for an 8-inch pot. For odd shapes and size, judgment should be used accordingly. A common error involves filling the pot so full of soil that there is no water space left.

The excess water that runs through into the gravel base will eventually be used up by capillarity into the soil above and/or through healthy roots extending down into the moist gravel.

Some very weak liquid food can be used for growing plants in such containers, but always less than in containers with drainage that permits a complete leaching through of possible excess soluble salts.

There will also be a more rapid accumulation of salt encrustation around the inside of the container at the surface of the soil where the water evaporates. Mainly for aesthetic reasons, this encrustation should be cleaned off periodically.

House plants always look better if grown together in a group, in a planter or bowl large enough to take several plants planted with due attention to the blending of foliage. They also thrive better together owing to the more humid conditions that the group maintains. Rather than plant them all directly in a large container, burying several pots in peat is again preferable. Then if you should want to change any one plant, you can do so easily without disturbing the roots of the other plants. As they come into season, flowering plants can be combined with the more permanent foliage plants.

In a greenhouse a moist atmosphere is maintained when desired by standing the plants on benches covered with sand, pea gravel, or some other moisture-retaining material kept saturated with water. In the home a similar method can be adopted, but it is not so convenient: the plants can be stood on a tray filled with perlite, moist sand, or vermiculite. This arrangement is best suited to the indoor windowsill devoted to plants.

Most plants growing indoors will grow toward the light. The one-sided growth can be counteracted by turning the plants occasionally, but with elaborate groups of plants in large containers this may not be an easy matter. In many public buildings where such displays are permanently planted supplementary lighting is often on the darker side of the plants. The extra lighting consists of a battery of high-power electric lamps mounted on a portable stand and brought into position at times when the public are not inconvenienced.

It is necessary to have the lights as close to the plants as possible in order to get the greatest benefit from them, because their power drops dramatically as the distance increases. But great care must be taken to avoid scorching the plants. Generally, ordinary incandescent lamps give off too much heat, and the heat from lights indoors does not dissipate rapidly as it does outdoors. Proper reflectors add greatly to the efficiency, and fluorescent tubes have a lower heat-to-candlepower ratio than do incandescent bulbs; therefore, they promote plant growth better.

In many houses, especially of the older type, there is insufficient window space, and it is often the dark corners that could most conveniently accommodate plants and benefit by them. Unfortunately, even plants from the shadiest forests are unlikely to survive for long if plunged into perpetual gloom indoors; but with the aid of electricity the darkest corners can be made cheerful with foliage, and even flowering plants. Containers can be fitted with a fluorescent lamp which, provided that it is not too far away from the plants, gives sufficient illumination to permit healthy growth without consuming much electricity. The plants chosen have to be limited to those that will not exceed about 18 inches in height, because artificial light must be fairly near. If the fluorescent lamp is put farther than about two feet from the plants the light intensity falls very greatly, and it would be necessary to use two adjacent lamps to provide enough illumination. Ordinary incandescent bulbs are virtually useless; fluorescent lamps give greater efficiency and do not radiate heat like incandescent bulbs. A fluorescent lamp is also a convenient shape for illuminating planters and the maximum light at minimum cost is obtained.

A simple way of adjusting lamp distances for plants is to

use an ordinary photographic exposure meter. The lamps should be put at a distance from the plants so that the reading on the meter matches a reading obtained in daylight. Since shade-loving plants will be grown under the artificial light, the meter reading for comparison should be taken on a cloudy day.

The fluorescent lamp should be carefully positioned over the planter and shaded to give a pleasing effect and to avoid dazzling the eye. The lamp itself should not be visible to the viewer in normal positions. Ferns, marantas, *Begonia rex*, peperomias and many other shade-loving plants will grow well under fluorescent lighting, but although the light may appear quite brilliant to the eye it is in fact very weak compared to the amount of light out of doors on a bright day.

African Violets *(Saintpaulia ionantha)* are especially suited to fluorescent lighting conditions, and special containers have been designed for them so that they can be had in flower nearly all the year round (Fig. 1). Saintpaulias enjoy a

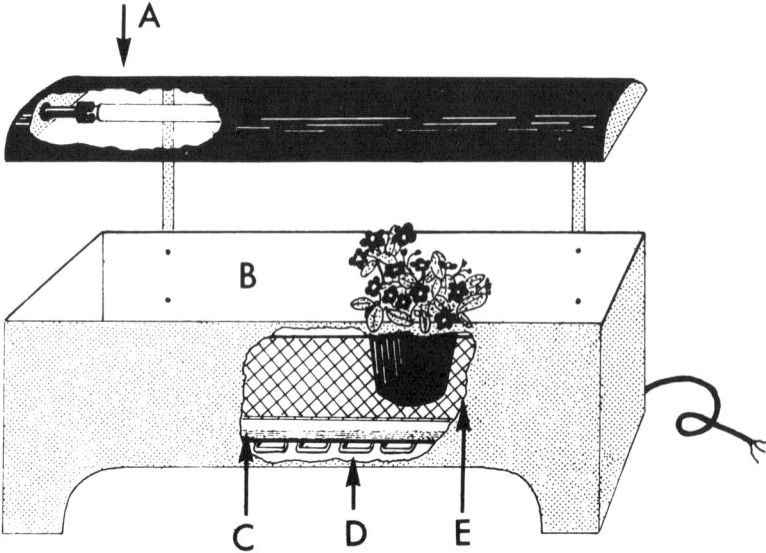

Fig. 1. Illuminated planter for growing African Violets: (A) fluorescent lamp; (B) planter; (C) water compartment; (D) heater; (E) grid on which pots stand.

warm humid atmosphere, and the planters have been designed so that moisture rising from slightly warmed water at the bottom rises around the plants standing on a grid just above the water. The fluorescent lamp radiates just sufficient gentle warmth to keep the plants growing nicely. There are now many beautiful varieties of saintpaulia with single and double flowers in various colors other than blue; these look delightful growing in an illuminated planter in what would otherwise be a dark corner of the room. It should not be overlooked that fluorescent lamps are available in circles and other shapes as well as tubes. The circles are especially useful for illuminating groups of plants arranged in ornamental pots, and when fitted with suitable shades, they make elegant plant lamps.

One point to be taken into account when illuminating flowers by fluorescent lamps is that some of the colors may look drab and unpleasant because the light wavelengths emitted are quite different from daylight. Reds, pinks, and blues are most affected, but yellows often appear brighter. It is possible to obtain special fluorescent lamps that are made for color matching, and these "matched" tubes should always be used when the correct and best rendering of color is desirable. Color balance can also be obtained by adding incandescent lights.

Plastic planters recently put on the market have built-in automatic watering that enables one to leave the plants without attention for weeks (Fig 2). The bottom of the planter contains a water reservoir that is filled by means of a removable funnel. It cannot be overfilled, because a vent pipe carries off excess water. The water is conveyed as needed to the soil in the upper part of the planter by means of nylon fabric wicks up which the water travels by capillary action. The soil is separated by a grid from the water reservoir at the bottom. Instead of soil, peat can be substituted and the potted plants buried in the peat, as already recommended. If this is done, the crocks covering the drainage hole at the bottom of the pots should be removed and a tuft of moist peat inserted. This

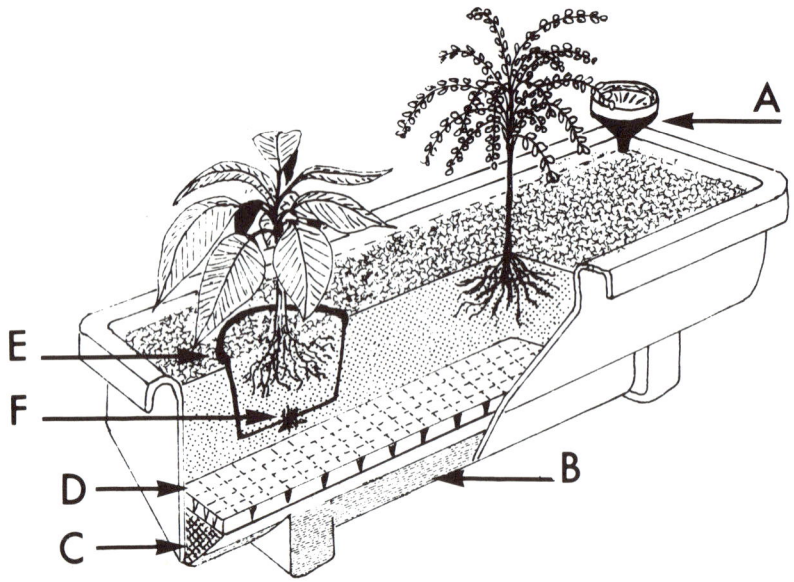

Fig. 2. The automatically watered planter: (A) removable funnel for filling water reservoir; (B) water reservoir; (C) nylon wick; (D) grid separating soil from the water; (E) pots can be buried in peat if desired, but if so they must be plugged with a tuft of peat substituted for the usual crock, as shown at (F), to convey the water into the pot.

allows water to be taken into the soil in the pot from the surrounding moist peat, which is in turn supplied with water from the reservoir. By standing these automatically watered planters in a warm place, or on a base slightly warmed with electric light bulbs, and giving them fluorescent illumination, they become ideal for growing saintpaulias.

So far we have seen how a number of problems concerning moisture, humidity, light, and to some extent temperature, can be overcome; but in a house where it is impossible to keep a reasonably steady temperature we are still unable to grow many exotic and interesting plants. To solve this supreme difficulty without the expense and installation of central heating, the plants can be accommodated in their own miniature greenhouse—an electrically warmed case, which can be illuminated if necessary.

Plant Cases

The growing of plants in cases is not a new idea. Wardian cases were used by the Victorians to grow ferns and similar plants requiring a humid atmosphere and warm, draft-free conditions (Fig. 3). The inventor was Nathaniel Bagshaw Ward, 1791-1868, who originally used glass cases to transport plants from abroad. The Wardian case of the Victorian drawing room was an elaborate and highly ornamental affair, but it had no means of heating built into it like its modern counterpart.

Modern plant cases are available in sizes to suit the surroundings and are constructed from noncorrodible metal, glass, and teak. In appearance they resemble large aquaria; they have sliding glass sides to give easy access, thermostatically controlled heating that can be adjusted to any desired temperature, provision for maintaining humidity, and usually fluorescent lighting. The base around the outside of the case is sufficiently deep to conceal pots from view, and with the aid of a little sphagnum moss and a few pieces of weathered rock, the plants can be given a pleasing natural

Fig. 3. The Victorian plant case was elaborately ornamented and was usually used to accommodate ferns. It was not heated.

12 GROWING EXOTIC PLANTS INDOORS

Plate 1. Terrarium containing orchids and exotic foliage plants. It is lighted by a fluorescent strip and thermostatically heated.

setting (Plate 1). The plant pots are stood on a tray, which forms the bottom of the case, and the tray contains a covering of moist sand or vermiculite to retain moisture. The tray is so designed that it is slightly smaller than the exterior casing. A slight gap between the tray and the walls of the case allows warm air to rise from the heaters below, thus providing ventilation and preventing the forming of condensation on the glass sides, which would obscure the plants from view (Fig. 4).

Plant cases can be put in a window where there is not too much direct sunshine and the illumination switched on only in the evening. If the case is to be put in a dark corner of the room, it will be necessary to leave the light on all day. In these circumstances, as pointed out earlier, the case should accommodate only shade-loving plants. By adjusting the sliding doors, the ventilation can be altered to give humidity to suit a wide range of plants.

Keeping Plants Healthy Indoors 13

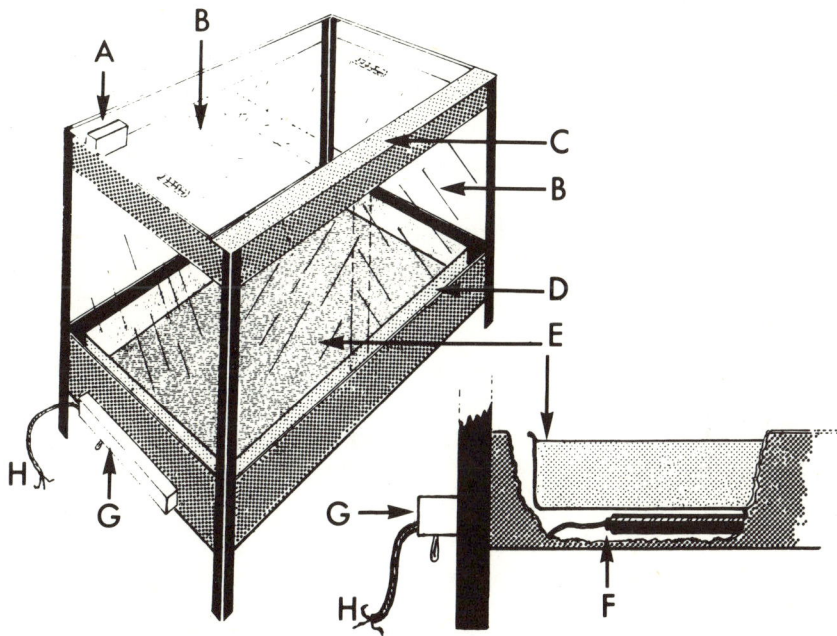

Fig. 4. Principles in the construction of the terrarium: (A) adjustable thermostat; (B) sliding glass doors; (C) reflector for fluorescent lighting strip; (D) space between the plant tray (E) and the case side to allow warm air to rise from the heater (F) helps to prevent misting of the glass; (G) control and switch for lighting unit; (H) electrical connection.

The handyman will find the construction of a plant case a simple matter, but it is doubtful whether the finished job will be as good or as cheap as the ready-made article when all the costs and the time spent are taken into account. The main advantage of making one's own is that it can be made to measure and to fit any desired space, whereas the commercial models are restricted to a very limited number of standard sizes. The materials of construction need very careful attention, and no ferrous metals (apart from stainless steel) or other easily corroded metals should be employed. Strong aluminum or zinc are the best choices, and these can be enameled with a hard-wearing enamel to give a professional finish. Zinc can be soldered easily, and aluminum can be easily joined (after roughening the surface) with the astonishingly strong, waterproof polymerizing adhesives that are now available. Special channeling can be obtained for sliding glass doors, which can be used for the side walls. Do not be tempted to use a transparent plastic like Lucite in place of glass. Plastic is much too soft and will become hopelessly abraded after a few cleanings. A thermostat will have to be provided and should be of the waterproof type used in greenhouses. Many different kinds are available, but the rod type is best. The thermostat should be fitted where it is concealed from the eye. There is no objection to putting it at the base provided that it is initially adjusted with reference to a thermometer placed in the body of the case.

If fluorescent lamps are to be fitted, it should be remembered that they are available in a limited number of standard lengths and the case dimensions may have to be adapted to fit them. Finally, it is absolutely essential to ground all electrical attachments and the case itself and to ensure that the electrical connections are made with proper care. Slapdash and makeshift electrical work on a job of this kind can result in fatal electric shocks.

The range of plants that can be grown in the heated case is limited only by their ultimate size and by the type of lighting used (i.e., natural or artificial). If the case gets a good deal of light from a window, almost any small-growing tropical or subtropical plant can be grown. If the thermostat is set at a lower temperature, a wide range of small, cool greenhouse plants will thrive. Orchids can be flowered very successfully—even the exotic, large-flowered cattleya orchids. Any of the plants in the following list will do well in a plant case:

Anthuriums (flowering)	*Biophytum sensitivum*
Fittonias	Ferns (small kinds)
Peperomias (many species)	*Tetranema mexicanum* (flowering)

Saintpaulias (flowering) Lobelia tenuior (flowering)
Marantas Baphia nitida
Selaginellas Mallotus philippinensis
Bertolonia marmorata Mimosa pudica
Pilea cadierei Dionaea muscipula

Plant Windows

The plant window can take a number of forms. In many countries it has become an important feature of house architecture and is often especially built-in for the purpose. In its simplest form it consists of an extra large thermopane window with the minimum amount of framework, if any. Inside, an extra large sill is provided and may be constructed in the form of a shallow trough complete with drain hole, allowing moist gravel to be distributed over the whole sill area. Ordinary windows can, of course, be converted to plant windows; but it is not advisable to do this in a room where there is only one window, because the conversion can impede ventilation and the plants are bound to reduce the amount of light entering the room.

Another type of plant window consists of an extra compartment built on to an existing window. (Figs. 5 and 6). With windows that open outwards, the construction of a plant window of this type means removing the whole of the existing frame, but sash windows can be left in place to form a kind of miniature conservatory that can be entirely cut off from the room. The structure should not be built to project too far from the outer wall or it may present an ungainly and obtrusive appearance when viewed from outside the house; the materials of construction should also be chosen to match the architecture of the house, but in all cases any shelving in the window is best made from plate glass. The roof of the plant window must be glass since that is one of the chief advantages of having a projecting window; it allows even overhead light for the plants, thereby preventing one-sided growth and improving the appearance of the plants from both sides of the window.

16 GROWING EXOTIC PLANTS INDOORS

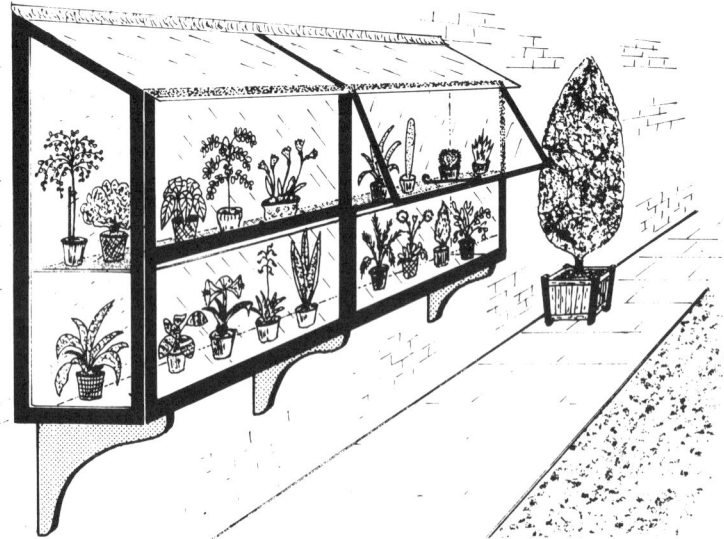

Fig. 5. Exterior of plant window.

Fig. 6. Interior of plant window with plate glass shelving.

Keeping Plants Healthy Indoors 17

Fig. 7. A large bay window fitted with plate glass shelves and French doors and converted into a plant room.

The plant window must be provided with adequate panes that can be opened for ventilation in summer, and for the winter it may be advisable to fit a small tubular electric heater to prevent plants from suffering from the cold. Plant windows of any description can also be plastic-lined in winter in the same way as greenhouses. The double "glazing" will also help to keep the room warm and prevent condensation and drip.

Bay windows can often be adapted to accommodate quite a large collection of plants. The roof of the bay is replaced with glass, and plate glass shelving is arranged around the interior. It may also be an advantage to divide the bay from the rest of the room by means of a glass partition fitted with a door or French doors. The bay is then, in effect, converted to a small conservatory (Fig. 7).

The Conservatory and Sun Porch

A conservatory or a sun porch is a delightful adjunct to a dwelling, but they are not the same thing. In the conservatory the comfort of the plants is given priority, whereas in the sun porch the plants take second place since it is essentially a room lived in by people. The same structure is usually suitable for both with little modification, but in the conservatory the atmosphere is kept more humid. In the sun porch, plants are treated more like ordinary room plants—although they will grow much better—and the air should be reasonably dry for comfort. There should also be plenty of space for suitable furniture. Plants for the sun porch can be grown in the various ornamental house plant containers already described. The sun porch is an ideal home for a warmed plant case and a bottle garden.

The conservatory, if used as it was in Victorian times, is essentially a place where plants are arranged for decorative effect. Originally, the plants were raised in greenhouses located in the garden and were brought into the conservatory as they came into season. The conservatory often had few plants growing permanently, other than some palms and climbers such as the magnificent bougainvillea. Nowadays it is rare for people to have a greenhouse, and the conservatory has to be used for a good deal of basic growing and propagating as well as for displaying the end product. In the Victorian era, when heating was cheap, the conservatory reached its peak of popularity, and some were amazingly elaborate. One of the most famous was constructed by Sir Henry Bessemer (the inventor of the steel-making process) in 1872 adjoining his house in Camberwell, London. The interior looked like a Moorish palace and was fitted with huge mirror walls to create an illusion of vastness. The mirrors were warmed from behind to prevent misting, and ornamental perforated panelling admitted heat from pipes beneath the tiled floor to warm the air of the conservatory (Plate 2). Today the comparatively small modern conservatory or sun porch can easily be added to a house and is fairly cheap to purchase:

Plate 2. An elaborate Victorian conservatory.

Plate 3. A modern sun porch.

ready-made sections are available that can be fitted together in a matter of a day or so (Plate 3). There are many different designs in materials ranging from anodized aluminum to redwood. A design that blends well with the architecture of the home must be chosen; otherwise a conservatory or sun porch can look an obtrusive misfit and very much out of place.

The roof of the sun room in Plate 3 is constructed of corrugated fiberglass panels. In recent years fiberglass panels have been especially produced for greenhouse use and are very superior for the growing of plants to the earlier fiberglass originally produced for sky lights and awnings.

Besides the new attributes of longer surface life, transmission of a greater range of light waves and percentage of light, and a much slower discoloration (some brands are guaranteed for twenty years), fiberglass, especially the corrugated, has good inherent structural strength that makes it feasible to use a less bulky and more attractive understructure.

Fiberglass is available in flat panels as well as corrugated. The flat panels are easier to install and more attractive for sidewalls than the corrugated. Although it is not generally as transparent as glass, it gives more privacy and makes a much better backstop for little ball players.

The pitch of a fiberglass roof with minimum understructure should be greater in areas of possible heavy snow loads, although this is ordinarily not a problem if the room is kept at a high enough temperature to melt the snow as it falls.

The floor of both a conservatory and a sun porch should be covered with a material that will not be damaged if water is spilled when watering the plants. Tiles are expensive, troublesome to put down and cold; but the new vinyl plastic flooring has none of these disadvantages. Good quality linoleum can be used but is less resistant. The basic flooring will probably be concrete, and this should be coated with a waterproofing preparation, of which several kinds are available, to prevent moisture rising up; this is especially important if a linoleum floor covering is to be put down, because damp below will cause mildew and rot. Much of the garden terrace furniture now sold in most of the large stores is ideal for a sun room, and includes wrought iron and wickerwork furniture which seems to go very well with a background of plants.

A sun porch constructed from ordinary glass is not much use for sunbathing; the short-wave radiations that cause suntan are absorbed by ordinary window glass. Special quartz glass transparent to ultraviolet light can be employed, but it is very expensive.

At the other extreme, it is possible to have privacy coupled with a more attractive structure and the elimination of sun glare, without resorting to shading, by using Solar Gray glass. The light transmission graduates from 42 percent, which is sufficient to grow many low light intensity plants, to 14 percent, which is not. With the 42 percent glass looking out during daylight hours is not noticeably impeded, while even at close range someone looking in can see only indistinct silhouettes.

Plants for a sun porch must be of a type that withstands a dry atmosphere and plenty of light, although if planted in suitable containers, the range of plants that can be grown is considerably increased. The sun porch is an ideal place for a plant case provided that the case is situated out of intense sunlight. The ample light and air of a sun porch also enable the following plants to be grown that are described in this book:

Acacias	Ficus benghalensis
Eucalyptus globulus	Fatsia japonica
Dracaena indivisa	Asparagus "ferns"
Grevillea robusta	Drosophyllum lusitanicum
Jacaranda mimosaefolia	Lophophora williamsii
Colchicums	Musa ensete
Ricinus communis	Sauromatum guttatum
Cannabis indica	Citrus mitis
Crocus sativus	Pelargoniums
Punica granatum	Miniature roses
Mimosa pudica	Dwarf conifers
	Everlasting flowers

In a conservatory can be grown nearly all the plants common to a cool greenhouse with a minimum winter temperature of 45-50° F. The conservatory, unlike the sun porch, must be shaded during the summer months to keep the many flowering plants in good condition.

Palms

Palms are especially suited to sun porch conditions and will be found to thrive. Contrary to common belief, most palms prefer plenty of light—not gloomy hotel foyers—and are rarely found in dense jungle. An airy sun porch with a translucent roof makes an ideal small private "palm court." No owner of such a pleasant adjunct to the home as a sun

Keeping Plants Healthy Indoors 23

porch, that can be kept at a minimum temperature of about 45° F. in winter, should be without a few representatives of the great and wonderful family of palms—the Palmaceae. It is true that most eventually grow to a considerable size, but there are several that remain conveniently small for many years. Palms lend an air of distinction to a conservatory or a sun porch. They are the aristocrats of the foliage plants and rank with the foremost in grace and elegance. Many of them are also fascinating because they are of great economic importance, and in their natural habitat provide an astonishing diversity of raw materials used commercially all over the world.

Copernica cerifera yields the hardest of all waxes, carnauba wax, which is incorporated in the best polishes for cars and furniture; the wax coats the leaves and is removed by shaking them. Sago, a starch used in foods and for stiffening fabrics, is obtained from *Caryota urens*, and a sugar is extracted from the sap. *Arenga saccharifera*, the Gomuti Palm, also gives a sugar and another type of sago together with a fiber used in making brushes and stuffing for upholstery. Most commercial sago comes from *Metroxylon rumphii* and *M. laeve*. The betel nut chewed by natives of India is the fruit of *Areca catechu* and in the powdered form is used as an intestinal worm repellent for domestic animals. The substance given the romantic name of "dragon's blood" is the dried resin of *Calamus draco (Daemonorops draco)* and is used for coloring varnishes. In Upper Egypt the Doum Palm, *Hyphaene thebaica*, is used for many purposes: the fruits are eaten and are said to taste like gingerbread, the seed is threaded to make rosaries, the wood is carved into ornaments and domestic utensils, and the leaves are fashioned into hats. Buttons, billiard balls and chessmen are made from vegetable ivory, which is the "nut" of *Phytelephas macrocarpa*. Various species of Raphia are the source of raffia, or bast, much used in handicrafts and for tying our plants in the garden. The gigantic Coco de Mer, which was found floating on the Indian Ocean long before its botanical

Plate 4. A coconut soon after germination.

source was known, is one of the largest nuts in the world, weighing about 40 pounds, and takes ten years to ripen; this is the fruit of *Lodoicea sechellarum*.

Probably the most curious of all palms is *Nipa fruticans*, of the Philippines and Ceylon. At one stage during its growth the brown bracts have the appearance of rubber hot-water bottles. What is more, they even *smell* like them, and get warm!—the warmth being evolved by chemical processes of metabolism during respiration of the young flowers. This type of palm was very prevalent in prehistoric times, and similar fruits to those of Nipa have been dug up in a fossilized state from the London Clay in the Thames.

The most familiar palm is, of course, the Coconut—*Cocos nucifera* (Plate 4). Coconut oil is used for soap making, in cosmetics, in confectionery, in margarines and cooking fats, in shampoos and in medicinal ointments. Doormats are made from coir, which is the fiber from the outer husk of the coconut, and upholstery is often stuffed with the same material. Desiccated coconut needs no introduction.

The Oil Palm, *Elaeis guineensis,* is another very important palm. The fruits yield palm kernel oil, used in soap manufacture and margarines, and it is also employed in the production of tin plate, from which cans and innumerable common objects are made.

This brief survey will, I hope, make the reader realize how fascinating palms can be. The majority of the economic palms can be seen only in the greenhouses of botanic gardens, but there are a few that can be grown quite easily by the amateur and a fair number that are valuable for their handsome foliage. The fact that some of the palms will grow to great heights in their natural habitat need not be a disadvantage, because the seeds of many are readily available and young plants can be freshly raised as necessary. They can be grown in pots for many years before reaching their true height.

Syagrus weddelliana (Cocos weddelliana), with its graceful fronds, is very effective as table decoration and can easily be obtained as a small potted plant. If raised from seed, a minimum winter temperature of about 50° F. is desirable. *Butia capitata (Cocos australis)* and *Butia yatay (Cocos yatay)* can be treated similarly. Two excellent house plants are *Howea belmoreana,* the Curly Palm, and *H. forsteriana,* known as Flat Palm, though both are often called Kentias in the florist trade. They will tolerate a winter temperature of about 45° F.

Many species of Phoenix are wonderful palms for the sun porch or conservatory with a winter temperature of about 50° F. *Phoenix dactylifera* is the Date Palm. It can be easily grown from date stones left over from the Christmas festivities and sown in spring in a warm propagating case. The Date Palm has been important since the earliest times, and the ceremony of pollination, during which the Arabs hang a spadix of male flowers over a spadix of female flowers, is recorded on Babylonian monuments. *Phoenix roebelinii,* the so-called Dwarf Date Palm, is a useful pot plant where space is limited.

Oreodoxa sancona is a common indoor palm. Other species are *O. oleracea,* the Cabbage Palm, so called because the heart leaves can be eaten, and O. regia, which has enormous beautiful feathery fronds. The Nikau Palm, also sometimes known as Cabbage Palm, is Rhapalostylis sapida (Areca sapida). This palm is of dwarf habit and is particularly suited to shade situations—probably happier in a conservatory than in a sun porch. Livistona chinensis, the Fan-leaved Palm, is another favorite house plant. This palm is easily raised from seed. Neanthe elegans (Chamaedorea elegans) is a small Mexican palm that can also be raised from seed and is the most commonly available palm in the United States. A palm requiring warmth but ideal for small pots is Archontophoenix cunninghamiana (Seaforthia elegans) (Fig. 8), which ultimately grows very tall but is a fine pot plant when raised from seed. For a conservatory or sun porch that can be kept just free from frost in winter the oriental Trachycarpus fortunei (Chamaerops excelsa) (Fig. 9) will be found quite hardy and can be grown from seed. It is also hardy in many places out of doors and produces flowers and fruit. Chamaerops humilis, commonly called Fan Palm, is distinctive in being the only palm native in Europe. It is fairly hardy and can be raised from seed. One of the loveliest palms, but unfortunately needing a fair amount of warmth, is Thrinax argentea, the Silver Thatch Palm. As the name implies, it has silvery fronds.

The Culture and Care of Palms in the Conservatory or Sun Porch

It will be seen from the descriptions just given that a great deal of warmth is not required for growing a number of beautiful palms. Although the potted plants are available from various nurseries, seed is an easy—and inexpensive—way to obtain them. The seed should be fairly freshly imported because in many cases it soon loses its viability, and where the seed is enclosed in a husk it should not be removed. Provided a high enough temperature can be attained, the seeds germinate easily in a propagating case, but in some cases germination may be slow and take several months. A

Keeping Plants Healthy Indoors 27

Fig. 8. *Archontophoenix cunninghamiana*, also known as *Seaforthia elegans*, is easy to raise from seed and is a handsome palm for small pots.

Fig. 9. *Trachycarpus fortunei*, also known as *Chamaerops excelsa*, is easy to grow from seed.

temperature of about 80° F. is usually sufficient. Even coconuts can be germinated; but it is, of course, necessary to acquire the complete nut and not just the kernel, which usually appears in the shops. The coconut also requires far too much warmth and space for the ordinary gardener. Palm seed should be sown in small pots of light, fibrous soil and barely covered.

Most palms require plenty of water—but at the same time perfect drainage. They prefer a slightly acid soil and pots which often *appear* far too small for them. Palms are especially susceptible to ill effects from root damage during repotting and the operation should be carried out with extra care. Various soils have been suggested, mostly based on fibrous loam, grit, or silica sand, and fibrous peat. A generous quantity of crushed charcoal should always be added.

In the days when palms were more commonly grown, it was a well-known practice to place a few crystals of ferrous sulphate (iron sulphate, or green vitriol) on the surface of the soil in the pot. This slowly dissolves during watering, keeps the soil acid, and improves the green color of the leaves. Only a few crystals should be used, since excess can be harmful.

When repotting a palm, a pot only slightly larger than the original should be employed, allowing about one to two inches of extra soil around the root ball.

During summer most palms benefit from occasional spray with rain water, but in a sun porch the fronds can be wiped with wet cotton, which will also keep them free from dust. A good liquid fertilizer is also beneficial. Potted palms grow best with their pots buried in moist peat, as described earlier.

Bottle Gardens

The idea of growing plants in bottles no doubt arose from the ship in the bottle, but the bottle is more important to the welfare of the plant than it is to the ship, since it keeps in moisture and humidity. In recent years bottle gardens have been given much publicity, although they are as old as the

Keeping Plants Healthy Indoors 29

Fig. 10. A narrow-necked bottle on its side and resting on wooden supports makes an attractive bottle garden but is more difficult to plant.

Wardian case (page 11). They are on sale in florists and exclusive stores at astonishingly high prices, and it is regrettable that so many of the bottles are so unsuitably planted that they are doomed to failure from the start. I have seen them planted with such subjects as sansevieria and cacti, which are bound to rot in the moist compost and atmosphere, and zebrina and helxine, which are so rampant that they will quickly smother any other plants and fill the bottle. Contrary to common belief, a bottle garden does need occasional attention. It also requires a carefully chosen position in the home where there is plenty of light—a sun porch is ideal—and very special care in selecting suitable subjects. The soil must not be too rich and it must be partially sterilized.

The Container

The most effective bottle gardens are in bottles, although many other containers, such as aquariums, large goblets, jars, and so forth, are often suggested. The bottle shape with narrow neck has decided advantages over other forms; the shape is aesthetically pleasing and the neck can be

Plate 5. A garden in a bottle.

Keeping Plants Healthy Indoors

plugged with cotton wool, which prevents ingress of pests and diseases.

The first step is to clean the container thoroughly. This is best done by rinsing with water, then with warm water containing detergent. Hot water should not be used or the glass may crack. Stubborn inside dirt can often be removed by adding torn newspaper and sand to the warm solution of detergent and swilling the pulpy mass around the bottle as vigorously as possible. After a final rinse in clean tap water, the bottle is ready for use.

The Soil Mix

A rich soil is undesirable for bottle gardens. The plants are selected for their slow growth and dwarf habit so that a plentiful supply of fertilizer is unnecessary and may promote growth that is too prolific. A light peat and perlite mix is suitable. To this is added a generous quantity of crushed charcoal, which serves to keep the soil from becoming sour. The soil must be properly sterilized because pests, diseases, and weed seeds can be an even greater nuisance in a bottle garden than normally.

The soil should be put into the bottle by means of a paper funnel; this prevents the soil from adhering to the wet sides. For a five-gallon bottle a depth of about four inches is sufficient. If the finished bottle will be viewed from all sides, the soil should be heaped slightly in the center so that the central larger plants will be raised and have a greater depth of soil. For one-sided viewing, the soil should be higher at the rear. Before adding the soil it should be thoroughly moistened —but it must not be wet. A layer of crushed charcoal at the bottom of the bottle, under the soil, aids drainage.

Planting

The planting of a bottle garden is a simple matter. The plants should have previously been grown in small pots so that they have a compact ball of roots with adhering soil. A simple tool usually recommended is an old teaspoon fastened

32   GROWING EXOTIC PLANTS INDOORS

Plate 6. A garden in a wide-mouthed jar.

to the end of a flat stick. This tool is used to dig the holes into which the plants are dropped after carefully passing them through the bottle neck. The spoon-stick is then used again to firm the soil around the plants. Sometimes a stick with a short length of stiff wire bent at a right angle fastened to the end is also useful. The roots of a plant can be hooked on to the wire and it is easier to lower and position the plant by means of the stick. When the plant is in the desired spot, the wire is unhooked by careful maneuvers of the stick.

The appearance of the garden can be greatly improved if a few pieces of weathered stone or weathered tree bark are included. To avoid the introduction of pests and diseases, stone and especially bark should be sterilized at 320° F. for two hours in an oven before introduction into the bottle. Great care must also be taken to see that the plants are healthy. Fungoid diseases can be particularly troublesome, and a bottle garden can be quickly destroyed by them. The worst enemy is Gray Mold *(Botrytis cinerea)*; this attacks damaged and dead parts of plants, from which it spreads to living tissues. Should the presence of even the smallest trace of Gray Mold be suspected—it has a grey furry appearance—the bottle should be fumigated.

After planting a bottle garden it is a good practice to plug the neck with cotton; this allows some change of air with expansion and contraction due to temperature variations, but pests and diseases are unable to enter.

When a bottle garden is put in a window, its symmetry may be upset because the plants will grow toward the light. This problem can be overcome by frequent turning, but in a sun porch the trouble will not be encountered.

Maintenance

The bottle garden rarely needs watering, but from time to time a few dead leaves may accumulate. These can be removed by piercing them with the wired stick used in planting. The plants may also require pruning occasionally, or even replacing if they become too large. A fragment of razor blade taped to a stick is useful for cutting off shoots and leaves.

Misting of the glass, which always occurs when the temperature inside the bottle is higher than that on the outside, can be avoided by keeping the room temperature as steady as possible and the bottle out of drafts. The bottle garden will need complete renewal of the soil and replanting after a time. The frequency depends on the type of plant and the rate of growth. Although plenty of light is essential to prevent weak spindly growth, direct sunlight is harmful and can seriously overheat the interior with resulting damage to the plants. Very low temperatures are undesirable because the plants are mostly from subtropical regions and will drop leaves and turn yellow in cold. High temperatures are likely to promote vigorous and rampant growth. Extremes should therefore be avoided, and ideally a temperature that just keeps a very slow rate of growth should be the object.

Plants

Obviously the plants chosen must be slow growing or have a dwarf habit. They must also prefer a high humidity and not suffer in shady conditions. Many common house plants are suitable, and a number that would normally only thrive in a greenhouse can also be employed. Preference is always given to attractive foliage, but a few flowering plants can be tried too. The following is a list of some that I have grown in bottles with considerable success:

Aregelia carolinae. Bromeliad
Calathea lubbersiana. Light and dark green tufted leaves
Cryptanthus aculis rubra. Bromeliad
Cryptanthus bivittatus. Bromeliad
Davallia mariesii. Dainty dwarf fern
Fittonia argyroneura. Striking white-veined green leaves
Maranta leuconeura. Pale green leaves, chocolate spots
Maranta l. massangeana. Pale green leaves, chocolate stripes
Pellionia daveauana. Trailing; brown and green oval leaves. Atrractive but a little fast growing
Peperomia caperata. Corrugated dark green leaves, white rat-tail flowers
Peperomia galloides. Dainty pale green whorls
Peperomia hederafolia. Pale olive green leaves with silver variegation; greenish catkins
Peperomia rubella. Tiny pale green leaves with silvery red markings on red stems
Peperomia sandersii. Spade-shaped leaves banded light and dark green on red stems
Pilea cadierei. Pale green leaves with silvery markings; a little fast growing
Saintpaulia ionantha. Various colored varieties; flowering
Selaginella species. Pretty moss-like growth, but can become rampant in warmth

Tetranema mexicanum. Small rosette of leaves, clusters of purple flowers on four-inch stems
Vriesia splendens major. Bromeliad

House Plants from Seed

A disadvantage with many house plants is that they are expensive if purchased as potted plants, but anyone with a small heated propagating case will be able to raise a number of fine and interesting house plants from seeds that cost only a few pennies. General hints on growing from seed are given in Chapter 5. Apart from the palms already described, the following house plants are well worth growing from seed.

Asparagus plumosus nana and *A. sprengeri,* often called Asparagus Ferns although they have absolutely no relationship to the ferns, are two of the most frequently seen and easily grown house plants. The former is a neat pot plant, and the latter is especially good for hanging baskets.

In extreme contrast to the finely divided foliage of the asparagus, *Fatsia japonica* has large glossy leaves. This plant is often known as *Aralia sieboldii,* which is a synonym, and sometimes it is quite incorrectly called Castor Oil Plant. Fatsia is very easy to grow and is near-hardy. It eventually becomes very large, and if planted out of doors will form an evergreen shrub about 10 feet high and bear large umbels of cream flowers in early winter in mild climates.

The "mimosa" of the florist is *Acacia dealbata.* This species makes a very attractive foliage plant when grown from seed, but it will not flower until it has reached a size inconvenient for most amateur conservatories. *A. brachybotrya* is a much lower-growing species, but for freedom of flowering *A. baileyana* is probably the best. *A. decora,* known as the Western Silver Wattle, and *A. discolor* are two more very fine species that do not grow excessively large. The acacias are very good for the dryish atmosphere and light conditions of a sun porch, but the roots must be kept moist. Many acacias are of considerable economic importance for their wood and gum. A species of acacia is believed to have been the source of the shittim wood of the Bible from which the Ark of the Covenant and the Tabernacle furniture were made.

Since few people realize that it is possible to grow coffee plants in the home, adding one to your collection of house plants can be relied upon to astonish visitors. The beans can be germinated in a propagating case at a temperature of about 80° F. and will grow throughout the year, although they rarely survive the winter unless they can be kept warm. The beans must be reasonably fresh, but some suppliers do not seem to realize that dried and shriveled beans are unlikely to be viable. The coffee plant *Coffea arabica* will not grow very large in amateur hands and is a good subject for the plant case; it has dark green glossy foliage. In a warm conservatory with a winter temperature of about 60° F. it will attain the size of a bush and produce white flowers.

Eucalyptus globulus is a good choice for the sun porch. Another especially good choice for a sun porch is *Dracaena indivisa (Cordyline indivisa)*. This plant has long, spiky, tapering leaves and is hardy out of doors in frost-free districts.

The Banyan tree, *Ficus benghalensis*, makes an interesting young foliage plant with dark green glossy leaves similar to *Ficus elastica*, the so-called Rubber Plant (most commercial rubber comes from *Hevea brasiliensis*). The Banyan tree is curious in that when fully grown it sends down adventitious roots from the branches. These roots form supporting pillars. In this way it spreads to cover an enormous amount of ground, and it is said that under one such tree an army of five thousand men have encamped. In India the tree is considered sacred. As a pot plant it needs to be kept warm in winter, and like all Ficus species the seeds need light for germination and should not be covered when sowing.

Two outstandingly beautiful foliage plants that should be in every collection of house plants are *Grevillea robusta* and *Jacaranda mimosaefolia;* both have graceful fern-like foliage and, although they grow to tree dimensions in their natural habitat, they can be kept as pot plants for many years by cutting them back. The former is calcifuge and should have the chalk omitted from the soil.

An unusual fern with interesting coloring is *Pellaea cordata*. The young leaflets have at first a red sheen which changes to green as they mature, when the leaf stalks turn yellow. Ferns are raised from spores and their treatment is dealt with briefly in Chapter 5. Most of the Philodendrons are good house plants, but few are easy to raise from seed. *P. bipinnatifidum* is an exception, and makes a handsome and impressive foliage plant with large, dark green, glossy leaves. This is another plant whose seeds require light for germination. *Schefflera digitata* somewhat resembles *Fatsia japonica,* but its leaves retain a delicate pale green color, whereas those of Fatsia darken with age. It is also slower growing and is not hardy, preferring a winter temperature of about 55° F.

Exacum affine (Gentianacae), commonly called Tiddly Winks, comes from the island of Socotra in the Arabian Sea. This plant can be grown from extremely fine seed that can be sown any month but generally in February for long summer and fall bloom. A tender, temperate greenhouse subject that cannot stand direct sun, *Exacum* is otherwise light tolerant. It is very self branching, with succulent leaves and many attractive and richly fragrant bright blue half-inch flowers with contrasting yellow stamens.

Many other plants described in this book can be raised from seed. Their suitability is brought to the reader's attention where appropriate.

Plate 7. A Zelkovia elm beginning its training as a Bonsai.

2

BONSAI

DWARF trees have been given considerable publicity in recent years and have captured the imagination of the public, probably because of the fine Japanese Bonsai exhibited at the major horticultural shows. Unfortunately this has led to much confusion and misunderstanding about the difference between natural dwarf trees, artificially dwarfed trees, and genuine Japanese Bonsai. This misunderstanding has also led to the exploitation of the public by unscrupulous commercial organizations through misleading advertisements. These advertisements have been so worded that readers have been made to believe that seeds of Bonsai are being made available. Many ordinary seeds of trees can be grown into Bonsai, but it takes probably at least twenty to fifty years of careful training and treatment to do it! Bonsai can, of course, be started from seed, but there is nothing special about the seed except that some species are more suitable for dwarfing than others. The seeds or seedlings of a number of ordinary woodland trees—gathered at absolutely no cost—can be grown into fine Bonsai if one has the patience. Various species of naturally dwarf trees and shrubs—especially those native to

China and Japan—are easier to train into Bonsai, and these are available from reputable suppliers at modest prices.

The substance of a plant consists of water, nitrogen, phosphorus, potassium, magnesium, and other trace elements derived from the soil, and carbon compounds such as cellulose, starches, and sugars, indirectly photosynthesized in the leaves from the carbon dioxide of the atmosphere. If circumstances are such that the supply of these nutrients is less than the plant's normal requirements, the plant becomes stunted. There are many instances in nature where plants struggle for existence on poor soils and, although unable to develop to full size, extract just sufficient nutriment to keep alive. Long-lived plants like trees and shrubs can exist for many years in such conditions and can be found on rocks, in the cracks of old walls, and even on roof tops. Such plants become attractively weathered over the passage of years, and those found growing on the mountain sides in Japan are often collected for growing as Bonsai. Branch and root pruning will reduce the plant's ability to obtain nutriment, even if a rich soil is available, and can therefore be employed artificially to produce dwarfing.

The word Bonsai means "planted in a shallow container" and is applied to trees grown in this way. The whole idea of Bonsai is to reproduce in perfect miniature the habit and mature appearance of a fully grown tree. A Bonsai should therefore appear to be very old, with weathered trunk, and often it is desirable for the branches to present a slightly distorted effect similar to that of old trees that have been exposed to the elements for centuries (Plates 7, 8, 9).

Dwarf trees were actually first grown in China, where they are called "p'en tsai," although the Chinese were more interested in training the plants to become strangely distorted and weird in appearance. The Japanese took up the art and developed Bonsai as we know them today. There are Japanese Bonsai in existence that are hundreds of years old and have been kept in the same family from generation to generation. Genuine Bonsai of this type are extremely expensive. How-

Plate 8. *Ginkgo biloba* being grown as a Bonsai.

ever, in recent years the Japanese have realized the commercial possibilities of Bonsai, and there are now many nurseries devoted to raising them for export as well as for sale in Japan. Other countries have also taken up the art. It should be realized that because of their great age genuine Bonsai can be only of oriental origin, the majority being Japanese. It should also be understood that the essential chracteristic of Bonsai is that they are old—at least twenty years of training is required to effect the necessary aged aesthetic appearance. Some of the naturally dwarf conifers can be grown to resemble Bonsai—at least to the inexperienced eye—but they are not Bonsai and it is unfortunate that people have occasionally been swindled into paying Bonsai prices for them.

Growing Bonsai

To grow Bonsai it is first necessary to select seeds of suitable subjects; or, as the Japanese often do, to find an already partially dwarfed specimen growing naturally for transplanting to a pot and training. Although almost any type of tree can be dwarfed, those with naturally small leaves give a more satisfying effect, since they will be in better proportion to the size of the Bonsai. Bonsai grown from fruiting or flowering trees such as malus or wistaria can be expected to produce flowers or fruits of correspondingly miniature proportions in due course. Some especially good plants to start as Bonsai are the following:

Acer buergerianum (Trident Maple)
Acer ginnala (Amur Maple)
Berberis thunbergii atropurpurea nana (Crimson Pygmy Barberry)
Buxus koreana microphylla (Wintergreen Boxwood)
Carissa grandiflora nana
Chaenomeles (Flowering Quince)
Crassula arborescens
Ginkgo biloba (Maidenhair Tree)
Juniperus chinensis
Juniperus procumbens (Japanese Juniper)
Picea abies nidiformis (Bird's Nest Spruce)
Picea glauca conica (Dwarf Alberta Spruce)
Picea glauca densata (Black Hill Spruce)
Picea glehni (Saghalin Spruce)
Pinus flexilis columnaris (Column Limber Pine)
Pinus mugho mughus (Mugho Pine)
Pinus nigra (Austrian Pine)
Pinus parviflora pentaphylla (Japanese White Pine)
Pinus sylvestris (Scotch Pine)
Pinus thunbergii (Japanese Black Pine)
Thuja occidentalis holmstrup (Holmstrup Arborvitae)

At first the germinated seedlings can be potted in ordinary small pots containing a medium mix of peat moss and sand with a little loam and stopped when they have reached the desired height to promote side growth at the top. This top growth will subsequently form the branches of the tree, and any lower growth from the "trunk" must be promptly removed. In the early stages, while the stem—later the trunk—is still supple, wires can be used to form it into a twisted shape, but care should be taken that the shape is one that a normal tree would acquire with age and not something grotesque. It is necessary to imagine what the stem will look like when it has thickened and formed a bark. Care must also be taken to ensure that the wires do not cut into the stem as the plant grows. Training of branches is accomplished by the use of further wires, tying, or hanging weights on them if the growth tends to be too upright.

Plate 9. A Bonsai Loquat with a fine trunk.

The early stages of training can be done in an ordinary small flower pot, but the time will come when a suitable dish or container will have to be found. Many of the best Bonsai pots are of Chinese origin, but any shallow ceramic pot will do, provided that it is well equipped with drainage holes and preferably unglazed inside—although the latter condition is not absolutely essential. Suitable containers specially made for the purpose are now available at modest prices.

At no time during the training or maintenance of Bonsai is a rich soil mix desirable, nor should strong fertilizers be used. However, the plant must not be starved, the whole idea being to provide sufficient nutriment to keep the plant healthy but not to encourage vigorous and lush growth. A mix of half peat and half sand or a mix of peat and sand with a little loam added has been used with considerable success, and an occasional sprinkling of bonemeal in spring is all that is needed in the way of fertilizer. Water, however, must never be lacking. Because of the small size of the containers in which Bonsai are grown, drying out is a common cause of failure, leading to deterioration and death of the plants. When the daily watering cannot be attended to, the container must be buried in moist peat; or, in cases of prolonged absence, the whole plant covered with a plastic bag to retain the moisture.

From time to time root pruning or repotting becomes necessary. This should be done when the plants are dormant, the best time being in very early spring just before growth begins. It is said that the Japanese often prune away about one-third of the root system, but this may be done over a period by constricting the roots with tightly wound wire—rather like applying a tourniquet—instead of cutting them, which causes loss of sap and possibly entry of disease organisms. Evergreen trees should be cautiously root pruned, if at all. During repotting and root pruning, as much as possible of the old soil should be removed without causing too much disturbance. On returning the plant to the container, potting must be firm. It is essential that the roots are once again surrounded by soil and that no air pockets are left.

The frequency of repotting and root pruning depends on the nature of the plant and the progress of training. It is impossible to give a precise indication of when it should be done—every two years is probably about average.

The aerial parts of the plant are pruned by careful cutting with a sharp razor blade, giving particular care to the trunk, where unwanted side shoots must be very promptly removed by cutting off flush.

The transference to a pot of a plant that is already dwarfed through growing on an unfavorable site can be hazardous, and again is best done during dormancy. It is astonishing how often such plants will die after removal from their natural home, even though they have been struggling for existence for many years. The trunk is often well developed and weathered on such plants, and only the branches need much training and shaping.

Displaying Bonsai

Most Bonsai are absolutely hardy and must spend the major part of their time out of doors. But even the hardy Bonsai will not suffer from brief visits indoors. As already mentioned, watering must be carefully attended to. Sometimes instead of growing Bonsai in dishes or pots, it may be better to grow them in a hollowed-out piece of porous rock. The hollow is filled with the soil mix and the rock stood in a tray with about an inch or so of water. This has the advantage of being self-watering, since the water is taken up into the rock by capillary action. Tufa or a porous sandstone is a suitable type of rock to use, and this method of growing Bonsai is particularly attractive because the rock soon becomes mossy, forming a "landscape" which enhances the effect of the tree.

The best site for Bonsai is an open but slightly sheltered position where excesses of wind, rain, and sun can be avoided. The Japanese place their Bonsai on tables near the house where they can be seen from inside, but they can also be kept in specially constructed Bonsai gardens. These con-

Fig. 11. Bonsai displayed in a shelter made from wooden slats.

sist of raised staging similar to that in a greenhouse, protected by a canopy of wooden slats (Fig. 11).

Extra precautions are needed during severe weather because the freezing of the wet soil might cause the pots to crack. To prevent this, surround the pots with peat, or if possible remove them temporarily to a cold greenhouse. Bonsai can, of course, be grown very well in the latter type of greenhouse where the temperature is kept only just above freezing during the winter.

3

TOUCH-SENSITIVE, MOTILE, AND CARNIVOROUS PLANTS

Movement in Plants

READERS of science fiction may have enjoyed the exciting novel by John Wyndham called *The Day of the Triffids*. In this story the Triffids are sinister plants that, owing to the development of the power of mobility, eventually take over mankind. All very farfetched you may think—but anyone who has stood in the quiet stillness of a greenhouse on a warm evening at sundown and watched the Telegraph Plant busily jerking its leaves will be less likely to sneer, as will anyone who has seen a spiked clam of a Venus's Flytrap snap shut on an unfortunate insect foolish enough to land on it or anyone who has been startled by touching a Sensitive Plant for the first time.

In general, plant movement is less spectacular than in the case of these three examples, but many plants do exhibit motility in some form other than by the ordinary process of growth.

Many people associate the power of movement only with animals, but that is quite erroneous. There are a fair number of animals that remain static all their life, particularly sea animals such as sea anemones, sponges, and corals. Conversely, there are numerous microscopic water plants of the algal and fungal type that can move at astonishing speeds. The speed is sometimes so great in proportion to their size that man would have to move at several hundred miles per hour to compete.

The mechanism of plant movement can be of several kinds. Microscopic water plants usually have special propelling organs, called flagella (because of their whip-like appearance), the movement of which is thought to be caused by the contraction of muscle-like strands very similar in composition to human muscle.

The movement of plants toward light—called phototropism—is due to the production within the plant of a growth-promoting substance known as auxin. Light reduces the concentration of auxin, with the result that, for example, in a plant placed on a windowsill the light side grows at a slower rate than the darker side. The greater number of stem cells created on the darker side causes the plant to bend toward the light. Gravity has a similar effect on plants —called geotropism—since it promotes an increase in the concentration of auxin on the lower side. Thus, if a plant is placed in a horizontal position, the growing point turns upward. That is why plants, seeds, and bulbs always find their way up through the soil even if accidentally placed upside-down. Auxins, or the so-called "plant hormones," have been extracted from plants and synthesized. In excessive doses they stimulate growth so much that the plant dies because it is unable to obtain nutriment fast enough. That is how most of the modern "hormone" weed killers work.

Temperature change is sometimes another cause of plant movement, especially the movement of certain spring flowers. The best known examples are the crocus and tulip; warmth quickly induces them to open their blooms and this is believed to be the result of accelerated growth of the cells lining the inside of the petals. However, some flowers may

Touch-Sensitive, Motile, and Carnivorous Plants 49

open or close in response to light changes, and the reason for this mechanism is often not at all clear. For example, mesembryanthemum and arctotis close their flowers at night or during dull weather; whereas nicotiana and the wonderfully fragrant calonyction only open at dusk or after dark.

Dehydration or the buildup of water pressure in plant cells is responsible for many of the more startling "explosions" of seed pods. The seed ejection of the Squirting Cucumber is due to high water pressure in some of the cells lining the interior of the fruit; in the pea family the seeds are scattered vigorously by the sudden release of tension due to dehydration of the pod. There are various plants that use similar methods for distributing pollen. One of the most spectacular of these is the aptly named Artillery Plant, *Pilea muscosa*, which suddenly releases its pollen as a puff of yellow "smoke."

The majority of plants that are of special interest because of the conspicuous movement of their leaves belong to the Leguminosae (the pea family). A smaller number are to be found in the Oxalidaceae. These plants are equipped with special groups of cells called pulvini (Plate 10), each pulvinus being located at the base of a leaf or leaf stalk. A pulvinus has a hydraulic mechanism that is not yet fully understood. It causes the leaf or stalk to move by its cells' swelling on filling with fluid and contracting on emptying. This special type of motility is called turgor action. It is also the causative agent of sleep movements in plants. Sleep movement is exhibited again by many of the Leguminosae: it is the closing down or folding together of the leaves at night, when the pulvini contract owing to a drop in water pressure. In a few cases the pulvini are touch-sensitive and bring about immediate and dramatic movement of the leaves or leaf stalks. In the Telegraph Plant, *Desmodium gyrans*, the pulvini expand and contract of their own accord continuously and so keep certain leaves in constant motion.

Jumping beans have long been a popular curiosity—but these are not an example of plant movement. The "beans" are

50 GROWING EXOTIC PLANTS INDOORS

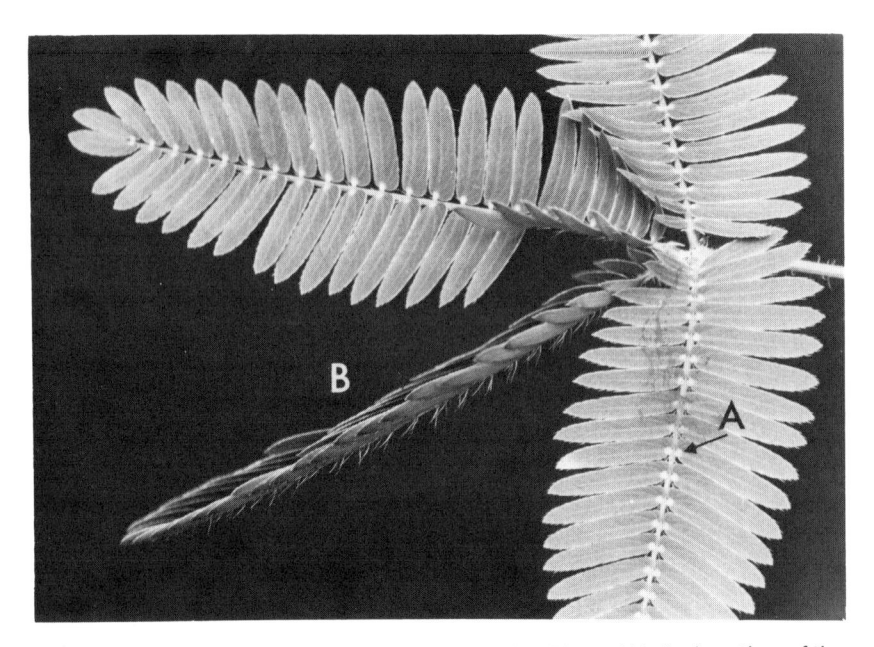

Plate 10. A close look at the leaf of the Sensitive Plant: (A) the location of the sensitive pulvinus; (B) a leaf that has closed after having been touched.

part of the fruit of a Mexican plant, *Stillingia palmeri,* and it is the twitching of a larva inside infected beans that causes the jumping.

Touch-Sensitive and Motile Plants for Pots

Mimosa Pudica. Leguminosae (Plates 10 and 11)

The Sensitive Plant is a name frequently given to this species, although the title rightfully belongs to *Mimosa sensitiva,* which is rather less sensitive. *Mimosa pudica* is, I think, one of the most intriguing of all plants and should be grown at some time by everyone interested in plant life. Few people remain unimpressed by its remarkable reaction to touch, and children are usually fascinated. It rarely fails to evoke an exclamation of astonishment from those who have never seen a touch-sensitive plant before.

Plate 11. The Sensitive Plant, *Mimosa pudica*, in flower.

The Sensitive Plant is a native of the tropics, where it is a perennial, but it can be easily grown as an annual from seed sown in May in the greenhouse or on a warm window sill. In fact it is better grown in this way, because although a perennial it is short-lived and is most sensitive as a young plant. Sow the seeds in a light soil mix and prick out the seedlings when large enough into small pots of the same soil mix. A final pot size of 3½ inches is quite suitable, and grown in this way the plants should reach a flowering size of about 9-12 inches in height by early autumn. Over-watering should be avoided and plenty of light provided; under glass, slight shading is advisable.

"Mimosa" of the florist is familiar to everyone; it is closely related to mimosa but belongs to a different genus and is actually *Acacia dealbata*. The Sensitive Plant bears flowers individually almost exactly similar in shape and size. However, only few of the fluffy balls are borne—not great clusters as in acacia—and their color is pale purple to pinkish (Plate 11). It is the leaves that are the interesting feature: they are pinnate (composed of a number of small leaves) and at the junction of each pair of pinnules is located a sensitive pulvinus (Plate 10). If this is carefully touched with a needle point, the pair will sharply close together. If the whole leaf is stroked down the center, where all the pinnules join they will close one after the other in a most peculiar manner. The same effect may be obtained by gently touching the end of the terminal leaf. A more violent tap causes all the pinnules to close together instantly, and since each leaf stalk also has a sensitive pulvinus where it joins the main stem, any general disturbance causes the whole plant to collapse in a most dramatic and striking way. The time that the plant takes to recover its normal appearance seems to vary considerably, but I find half an hour or so about average.

The seeds are fairly large and usually germinate well. In case of difficulty it may help to soak them overnight before sowing. When grown as an annual it is unnecessary to apply fertilizers at any stage.

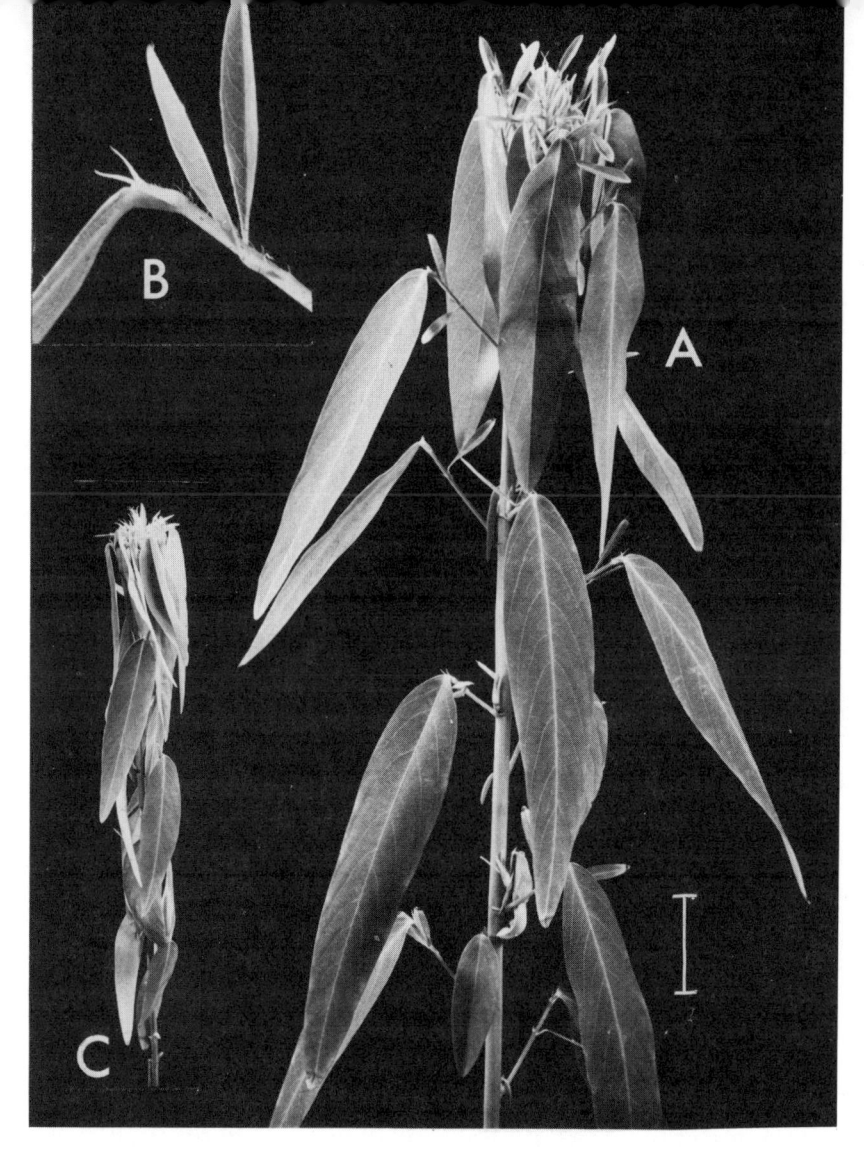

Plate 12. The Telegraph Plant, *Desmodium gyrans:* (A) the general habit of the plant; (B) a close look at a motile pair of leaves; (C) the leaves folded down at night.

Desmodium Gyrans. Leguminosae (Plate 12)

Like those of the Sensitive Plant, the leaves of *Desmodium gyrans* are motile—but there is no need to touch them. It is certainly a very weird subject and is of great educational value, because the particular type of plant movement it demonstrates is probably unique.

Again the plant is tropical in origin and is usually described as a hothouse annual. This misleading information often deters people from trying to grow it, since few gardeners can maintain the plants at hothouse temperatures; but the plants can be raised perfectly well with no extra heating in an ordinary greenhouse during the warmer months of the year. If no greenhouse is available, it may be worth experimenting with them on a warm windowsill indoors, but I must confess that I have not tried them in such conditions myself. The plants seem to grow with little trouble—the difficulty is in obtaining viable seeds and germinating them. In my experience the seeds must be reasonably fresh, and I fear that seed suppliers have sometimes supplied seeds that are absolutely nonviable. The seeds are about an eighth of an inch long; if examined carefully, some may be found to be greenish and others black. In my experiments the green seeds germinated within three to eight days at 86° F., but the black ones took much longer or failed to germinate. The seeds can be germinated in a warm propagating case or by means of one of the special contrivances suggested in Chapter 5. I place the seeds on a pad of cotton wool for germination, and as soon as they start to germinate I transfer them to small pots of a medium soil mix contained in a propagator at about 68° F. If the germination can be carried out from about March to May, quite substantial plants will be had by autumn. A 3½-inch pot is adequate for the final pot size.

I prefer to let the plants grow naturally. In the majority of cases they form a single stem, although sometimes branching does occur. Branching can be induced, if desired, by stopping the plants when they are about six inches high.

The leaves of *D. gyrans* are trifoliate, consisting of one large terminal leaf with two small laterals at the base (Plate 12, B). It is the laterals that exhibit the extraordinary movement that gives this species the common name of Telegraph or Semaphore Plant; but young seedlings do not form laterals, and the plant should be given a chance to grow and develop properly before one can expect to observe leaf motion. The peculiar movement of the lateral leaves, sometimes of a jerking nature, gives the impression that they are signalling like a semaphore. It is often written that bright sunshine is necessary to promote the motion, but plants I have grown have moved quite agitatedly at dusk. However, a high temperature does help, and the best display is to be seen on a very warm summer's day. If the leaves are carefully watched, it will be noticed that each moves in an elliptical orbit, sometimes folding together when they meet and afterwards springing apart.

The Telegraph Plant is also excellent for an example of sleep movement: at night all the leaves fold down close to the stem and the plant appears to stand at attention (Plate 12, C).

If conditions are favorable, violet pea-like flowers are produced in early autumn, but the plants often fail to flower at low temperatures.

Other Sensitive Plants

Several other plants are markedly touch-sensitive but are less easy to grow or obtain. One of the most reactive is *Neptunia oleraceae* (Plate 13), which is a tropical aquatic. Its leaves are very similar to those of *Mimosa pudica* and behave in the same manner. This plant is often grown in the tropical water-lily ponds of botanic gardens and is well worth watching for.

Biophytum sensitivum (Oxalis sensitiva) (Plate 14) belongs to the Oxalidaceae (the oxalis family) and forms attractive neat rosettes of leaves, reaching only about 5 inches in height. This plant grows in a number of warm countries and in its natural habitat the leaves are outstandingly sensitive. Many travelers enjoy telling stories of how the ground appears to move at the slightest disturbance, owing to leaf closure being transmitted throughout the entire plant colony. However, when they are grown in the greenhouse I have often found them disappointingly insensitive. A warm greenhouse or propagating case is essential if the plant is to survive the winter, but given such conditions it is easy to

Plate 13. The aquatic *Neptunia oleraceae* has very sensitive leaves similar to those of the Sensitive Plant.

grow from seed or root cuttings. Small yellow flowers are produced during summer.

Mimosa sensitiva has already been mentioned, but it is very much less sensitive than M. pudica and is not easy to obtain.

A quite hardy sensitive plant is Morongia uncinata. This plant has leaves exactly like M. pudica and is fairly sensitive, but I find it very slow growing indeed.

Although many explanations have been put forward in an attempt to account for the movement of touch-sensitive and motile plants, no one knows why these plants have evolved in such a manner, and it provides an excellent subject for speculation and discussion. The exact mechanism of the structures controlling the movement also remains extremely obscure and still needs a great deal of scientific investigation.

Plate 14. *Biophytum sensitivum* forms neat rosettes of sensitive leaves.

The Nature of Carnivorous or Insectivorous Plants

Writers of adventure stories have from time to time described man-eating plants in great detail, and it has not always been clear whether one is expected to believe in their existence. Certainly there is little evidence that such terrestrial plants are factual, but all the mysteries of the ocean bed have yet to be learned, and it is quite likely that there are some plants of the sea-anemone type large enough to entangle and digest a man-sized animal. However, plants capable of trapping and digesting small insects are very real indeed and are exceptionally interesting to grow—particularly if one has a taste for the macabre!

Some plants, such as *Aristolochia elegans*, trap insects for a short period sufficient for the captive in struggling to escape to become dusted with pollen or to deposit it on the plant. When the insect has served its purpose it is in some cases allowed to go free owing to a change in the structure of the trap forming a way of escape. Plants of this kind cannot be classed as carnivorous.

The true carnivorous plants mostly belong to five families probably unfamiliar to most gardeners: Cephalotaceae, Droseraceae, Lentibulariaceae, Nepenthaceae and Sarraceniaceae. The members of these families employ several devices for catching their prey. A few have a mechanical trap—a variation of the mousetrap principle—which is sensitive to touch and springs shut on any creature that alights on it (Fig. 13); the trap operates by turgor action, described on page 49. Some people have suggested that these plants exude an odor that lures the prey to the trap, but from my own observations I am doubtful about this. Other plants have no rapid motile means of trapping but rely on a sticky secretion in the same way as the old-fashioned flypaper. However, in these plants the adhesive secretion is usually on the surface of numerous hairs which are motile. As soon as the insect is caught, the hairs slowly enfold the victim, and a further secretion of the plant's digestive juices takes place (Plate 15). When the insect is digested and absorbed, the hairs unfold to their normal position and await the next meal.

Many of the most attractive carnivorous plants, such as the pitcher plants, employ quite different means of securing their prey. In these the victim is deceived by the physical structure of the trap, which is usually funnel- or pitcher-shaped (Plate 18). The inside walls may either be coated with a secretion that the legs of the creature are unable to grip, or the walls may be equipped with down-pointing hairs or other structures making exit impossible. Occasionally the funnel may be shaped to make entrance easy but exit difficult, rather in the manner of an unspillable inkwell—but in all cases the victim is disposed of by the "acid-bath murder" technique. At the bottom of the pitcher or funnel is a pool of digestive liquid into which the prey eventually falls and is dissolved.

Touch-Sensitive, Motile, and Carnivorous Plants

Plate 15. A close look at the sticky hairs on the leaves of Drosera that catch and digest insects.

In describing the carnivorous plants I have used the word *insect* loosely to cover all the creatures commonly known to the ordinary gardener by that name; but although the diet of the plants consists chiefly of flies and other true members of the Insecta, they also catch spiders, small crustaceans, and other animals that are not insects.

A large number of the carnivorous plants grow in moist places or on soil of low nitrogen content. Their carnivorous nature, therefore, probably evolved as a means of supplying supplementary nitrogen for nutrition; but it should not be thought that the plants are dependent on their catch—they grow perfectly well if no insects are available. When cultivating the plants there is no need to feed them via their digestive traps, although they will take and absorb tiny fragments of meat with advantage. Ordinary fertilizers are absorbed by the roots in the normal way, and I have reason to believe that foliar fertilizers are particularly effective, especially in the case of the Nepenthaceae.

The process of digestion in the carnivorous plants is extremely interesting, and although it has been carefully studied by a number of scientists, the exact chemical processes involved are far from being fully understood. However, it is known that one or more enzymes are largely responsible. An enzyme is an organic chemical compound, usually of considerable complexity, that instigates a chemical reaction between substances that may not normally be reactive. This is better understood by quoting the typical example of starch and water: if a small quantity of an enzyme called amylase is added to a solution of starch the starch is acted upon by the water and converted into glucose. In the very complicated workings of living creatures many different enzymes are needed to initiate the various chemical processes of metabolism. The enzymes produced by the carnivorous plants are called proteolytic enzymes because they enable water, and other chemicals formed by the plant, to digest (or break down into simple substances) the nitrogen-containing proteins of which their prey is mainly composed. These enzymes are very similar to those formed in the human stomach for exactly the same purpose, and they will digest meat just as well. If a fragment of meat is dropped into the liquid at the bottom of a pitcher plant, it will slowly disappear in a matter of hours or days, depending on the size of the fragment and the activity of the enzymic liquid at the time. The protein of the meat is converted into simpler compounds, which dissolve in the liquid and are absorbed by the plant through the walls of the pitcher. In the case of plants like the Venus's Flytrap or the sticky-haired droseras, the digestive liquefying enzymes are secreted by the walls of the trap or by the hairs.

A practical use of the proteolytic enzymes is in the so-called meat-tenderizing salt nowadays so useful in the kitchen. The enzymes used are usually bromelian, obtained from the pineapple plant; papain, extracted from the latex of

Touch-Sensitive, Motile, and Carnivorous Plants

the papaw *(Carica papaya)*; or ficin, prepared from fig-tree latex *(Ficus carica)*. If the tenderizing salt is used too generously, the meat can be spoiled for eating by becoming too pappy or almost liquid.

Some very fascinating experiments have recently been carried out on the pitcher plants. The experiments emphasize how similar they are to an animal stomach and show how they can be made "hungry" by the same digestion-promoting chemical substances. When we have a feeling of hunger, it is associated with the secretion of stomach acid (hydrochloric acid), which can be stimulated by a substance called histamine. An acid solution is also necessary to the digestion of pitcher plants, but full acidity of the liquid at the bottom of the pitchers is attained only on maturity. If a fragment of meat is added to an immature pitcher nothing happens; but if histamine is also added, first the acidity and then the enzymic activity rapidly rise, whereupon the meat is quickly digested.

Although the digestive power of the enzymes is considerable, it is a strange fact that a few insects are able to resist it completely and even make use of the liquid in the pitchers as a medium for the development of a stage in their life cycle. Presumably these creatures are capable of secreting a substance that inhibits proteolytic enzyme action. The liquid in the pitchers is not poisonous, and there are numerous tales of travelers quenching their thirst from them.

It will be noticed that many of the pitchers or funnels of the pitcher plants have lid-like appendages. These seem to take no part in trapping prey. Their function appears to be to prevent rain water from entering the trap and diluting the digestive fluid.

Culture of Carnivorous Plants

Few of the carnivorous plants are difficult to grow provided that their sometimes exacting requirements are given attention. Many of our common decorative garden plants grow happily in conditions very different from their natural habitat, but in general this is not so with the carnivorous plants—they are much more fussy, and it pays to study their natural environment carefully.

With few exceptions a very humid atmosphere around the plant is most important, but not all the carnivorous plants need an exceptionally high temperature and some are quite hardy. In a greenhouse it is usually not difficult to arrange a high humidity. However, if only a few carnivorous plants are being grown, it is not always desirable for other plants sharing the greenhouse. Humid conditions are also important if the carnivorous plants are to be grown indoors on a windowsill. In such cases a local moist atmosphere must be provided by means of a glass cover over the plant. This can be a cloche with the ends covered in with glass, a large bottle with the bottom cut off, or a bell jar. The Victorian glass domes used to cover stuffed birds, wax flowers, etc., can sometimes be acquired from secondhand shops and these are very useful. The electrically warmed and illuminated houseplant cases described in Chapter 1 are, of course, ideal for tender carnivorous plants.

The moisture under the cover or around the plants is maintained by standing them on a tray or in a dish containing water-saturated peat, moss, or fine sand.

Nearly all carnivorous plants should be watered with *rain water* or other soft water since they are calcifuge plants and will deteriorate in the presence of lime. In most cases a special moisture-retaining soil mix is needed which is made up from peat, sphagnum moss, sand, and charcoal. Living sphagnum moss is normally used, especially for seed sowing. The seed is sown so that it falls between the moss which is growing in the pan. Incidentally, sphagnum moss also goes brown and dies if watered with limy water. Other methods of propagation of carnivorous plants will be described under their respective headings.

Since the majority do not grow in rich soils, the ordinary fertilizers should be applied with caution, if at all. Bonemeal is probably the safest, but even this should be used sparingly.

The Cephalotaceae

Cephalotus follicularis (Fig. 12) is the only plant in this family and is often known as the Australian Pitcher Plant, since it is a native of the marshes in Western Australia. It is low growing, reaching a height of about 5 inches, and bears clusters of small white flowers. The flowers are of no particular interest, but the charming pitchers make this plant alluring and decorative and are similar in appearance to those borne by the Nepenthaceae.

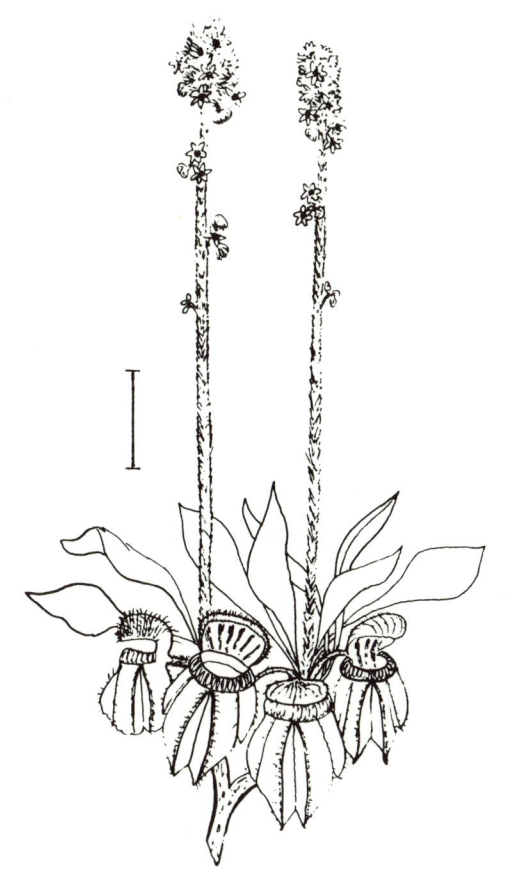

Fig. 12. *Cephalotus follicularis*, the Australian Pitcher Plant.

Abundant moisture is essential to cephalotus; a soil mix consisting of equal parts of peat and sphagnum moss with some crushed charcoal and very little bonemeal is usually satisfactory. The soil should be contained in a half-pot, which is immersed to the rim in soaked sphagnum or other moisture-retaining material. The pot should be covered with a bell jar or a moist atmosphere secured in some other way. During winter the plants are dormant and can safely be allowed to become slightly drier, but at no time must they dry out completely.

A minimum winter temperature of about 50° F. is desirable, and plenty of light should be given at all times. However, if grown under a bell jar or glass cover of small dimensions, direct sunlight should be avoided.

Cephalotus can be grown from seed, which must be fairly fresh, sown on the soil mix described, and it can be propagated by division of the plant when in active growth. Early spring is the best time for seed sowing. Cephalotus is unfortunately rare and difficult to obtain.

The Droseraceae

The three genera of this family that we shall consider here are Drosera, Dionaea, and Drosophyllum; these are all low growing and catch their prey by means of sticky hairs on their leaves.

Drosera rotundifolia, the Round-leaved Sundew, is hardy and commonly found growing wild in various parts of Great Britain. Prepared as an infusion, it was an old herbal remedy for coughs, and the fresh juice was reputed to be effective as a treatment for warts and corns. It is a small plant, bearing white flowers, and can easily be grown in pans of a very moist peaty soil, but it is by no means showy. *D. longifolia* and *D. angelica* are similar but have longer leaves.

Three good greenhouse species are the Australian *D. binata,* with white flowers (Plate 16), and the South African *D. capensis* and Australian *D. spathulata,* both with purple flowers. All these require a minimum winter temperature of

Plate 16. The attractive flowers of *Drosera binata* are unexpected in such a sinister plant.

about 45° F. and can be grown in the amateur greenhouse or conservatory. The usual mixture of living sphagnum moss and peat with added charcoal should be used in half-pots standing in a pan of water. The whole should then be covered with a bell jar or similar container.

Droseras can be propagated from fresh seed sown on sphagnum moss (as described under Cephalotus) or by root division during early spring. *D. binata* is best raised from root cuttings about ½ inch long and laid horizontally about ¼ inch deep in a peat/sand mixture. When an inch or so of top growth has been made, the plants can be transferred to the permanent sphagnum/peat mixture.

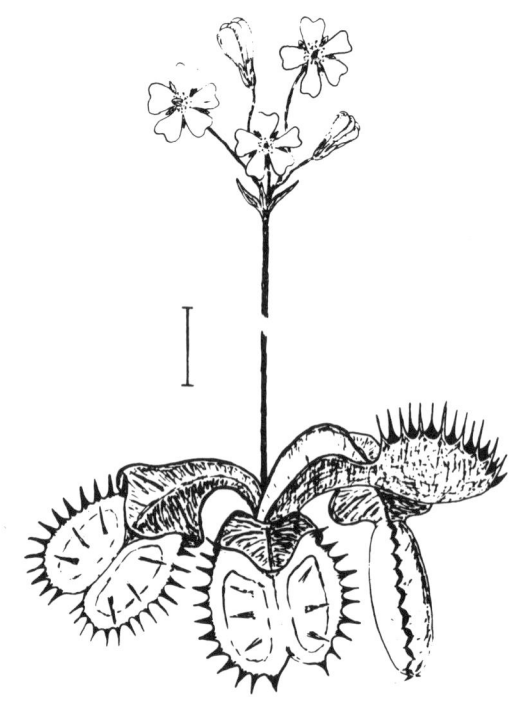

Fig. 13. *Dionaea muscipula,* Venus's Flytrap.

The most publicized member of the Droseraceae is Venus's Flytrap, *Dionaea muscipula* (Fig. 13); this is the plant with touch-sensitive traps shaped like toothed clams. The trap is set off by any disturbance of the sensitive spines, of which there are three in each clam, but sometimes even touching the outside will cause them to close. It is curious that at low temperatures the sensitive spines must be touched twice in rapid succession to have an effect; the time interval seems to be about 2-20 seconds.

From time to time so-called "bulbs" or "bulbils" of this plant are advertised in the press and given misleading publicity. These "bulbils" are really root crowns. The crown should be planted so that the top just protrudes from the surface of the soil, which should be of the type already described but with a good proportion of clean washed sand added. A peat/vermiculite/charcoal mixture can also be used. The crowns often rot, and better, stronger plants are usually raised from seed—which, however, is less easy to obtain. Seed should be sown as described under Cephalotus and should be reasonably fresh for good germination.

Venus's Flytrap needs a minimum winter temperature of about 55° F., but since the plant is quite low growing it can be kept very well in a small propagating case. An indoor case is not suitable unless it is in a very light position. *D. muscipula* deteriorates in the shade, and the color of the traps, which should be greenish red, fades or turns yellow. Like all the carnivorous plants so far described it must have a moist atmosphere, and a bell jar is again necessary if a humid greenhouse is not available. In this case some ventilation should be allowed by raising the cover an inch or so on suitable supports. The half-pot containing the plants should stand in half an inch or so of water.

White flowers may appear during summer, and when the plants are actively growing they can sometimes be further propagated by layering the leaves; new plants may form at the margins.

Drosophyllum lusitanicum is the only species of the genus, and although it belongs to the Droseraceae its cultural requirements are quite different from those of the other plants described. Its leaves are also devoid of any self-movement but have sticky hairs and are similar in appearance to the droseras. With *D. lusitanicum* an atmosphere too moist should be avoided since the plant is a native of Portugal, Southern Spain, and Morocco. Peat and perlite with a good proportion of washed sand added seems to be a suitable soil mix. A sunny position and a minimum winter temperature of about 50-55° F. are desirable. The plant can be raised from seed and bears large yellow flowers on low stems during summer.

A characteristic of the Droseraceae is that the young leaves are circinnate (coiled as in the ferns), which is very rare in the flowering plants.

The Lentibulariaceae

Pinguicula vulgaris is the British Butterwort; it has attractive rosettes of yellowish succulent leaves whose glossy sheen, common to many of the pinguicula species, has given rise to the name Butterwort. From the center of the rosette purplish stalks arise during May to July and bear small violet flowers. Another hardy species is *P. grandiflora,* which is a good plant for the bog garden. This plant has large blue flowers. Both can be grown in pans of moist peaty soil. The juice of some species has been used for curdling milk and as a household treatment for wounds.

The pinguicula most frequently grown under glass is *P. bakeriana (P. caudata)* (Plate 17), which is indigenous to Mexico and bears flowers of a very beautiful rich magenta color becoming paler as the flower ages. During winter this

Plate 17. The insectivorous *Pinguicula bakeriana* in flower.

species needs a minimum temperature of about 50° F. and should be allowed to become drier; but in summer it requires the very moist conditions described for most of the other carnivorous plants, although in the greenhouse a cover is not usually necessary.

It is an advantage to add some sterilized loam to the soil mix for this plant: one part loam, one part washed fine sand, three parts peat, a quarter part charcoal, and a quarter part sphagnum moss to keep the texture open. The species can be raised from seed and propagated from leaf cuttings taken during summer. The cuttings should be laid flat on the surface of the soil and covered with a bell jar.

Water should be kept off the leaves of pinguiculas because it sometimes spoils their attractive sheen.

Utricularia species are mostly aquatics, with strange bladders in which insects are trapped, but some are terrestrial, and a few are epiphytic trailing plants. In general the most decorative utricularias require very warm and moist conditions, difficult for the amateur to maintain, and are best suited to the greenhouses of botanic gardens.

However, the common bladderwort (*Utricularia vulgaris*) (Fig. 14) is a hardy aquatic that can be found in still or slow-moving waters. It can be grown in aquariums and is of special interest because of the extraordinary and complex mechanism of its traps. At the entrance of these bladder traps, which are less than ¼ inch long, are located sensitive hairs. The entrance is normally closed, but if the hairs are touched by an aquatic insect it opens with astonishing speed, and at the same time the bladder expands. The powerful suction produced sweeps the unfortunate victim inside the bladder, which instantly closes. This sequence of events takes only about one-thirtieth of a second. The detail of the mechanism and the structure of the tiny trap are exceedingly complicated. For many years its operation and how the insects got inside the trap was a complete puzzle to observers. The fraction of a second in which the whole operation takes place is much too fast for the human eye to register. *U. vul-*

70 GROWING EXOTIC PLANTS INDOORS

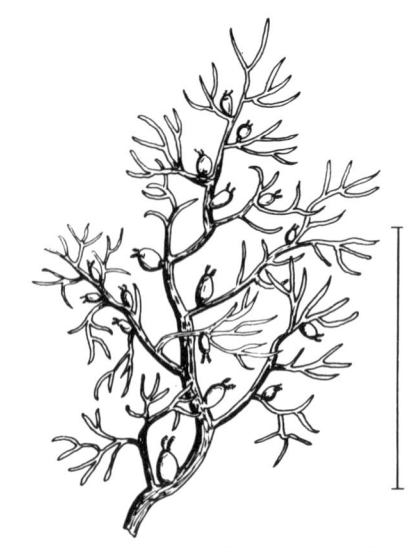

Fig. 14. *Utricularia vulgaris,* common Bladderwort.

garis produces small yellow flowers, which rise a few inches above the surface of the water. After flowering, the plant submerges.

The Nepenthaceae

Nepenthes, the Pitcher Plant genus, is the only one in this family, but it has about sixty species. All bear the quaint pitchers that make them so attractive and fascinating to grow, but many amateur gardeners will not be able to maintain the high winter temperatures necessary. A minimum winter temperature of about 60° F. is essential, and a number of the species require at least 70° F. However, those enterprising gardeners with a greenhouse equipped with a large high-temperature case should be able to grow the smaller species without too much difficulty. Those gardeners who do not think that they will be able to cope may nevertheless find the cultural details interesting.

Nepenthes do not flower generously, but seed does appear on the market from time to time, the commonest being that of *Nepenthes khasiana*. There are many hybrids, and a number of old favorite species such as *N. rafflesiana* and *N. hookeriana*, which were much grown by the Victorians. It is not much use giving detailed descriptions of many species, because nowadays we usually have to be grateful for anything that we can acquire or scrounge.

Seed should be sown during summer at a temperature of about 86° F. in the sphagnum moss-type mixture already mentioned. The pans should be in a closed propagating case and the seedlings pricked out into small pots of the same soil mix when large enough. When sufficient growth has been made, they should be further transferred to orchid baskets (made from teak slats) and suspended from the roof of the greenhouse or heated plant case so as to give them plenty of light—but not direct sunlight in the early stages. The soil mixes used differ according to the preferences of various growers, but an example is a mixture of about equal parts of sphagnum moss, sterilized loam, peat, and sharp sand. To this can be added charcoal, a little bonemeal, and some broken pot to keep the soil well aerated. The sphagnum moss can be sterilized with boiling water with advantage, since there is no need for it to be living. Cow manure has been used as a fertilizer with apparent beneficial effect, but the odor that permeates the greenhouse as a result is really dreadful. Ordinary organic-type liquid fertilizers are odorless and do just as well. I think the foliar feeds are also very good if well diluted.

As the plants continue to grow, the wire supports of the baskets should be lengthened so as to keep the tops of the plants fairly near the glass and out of the shade that might be cast by other plants or the greenhouse structure. There is considerable disagreement about the amount of light that should be allowed to reach pitcher plants. Some gardeners claim that the house should be well shaded, and others insist that plenty of light is necessary for the generous formation of pitchers. I support the latter school and think that only very slight shade is needed during prolonged sunny weather. However, it is important—as when growing any plant—that sudden

72 GROWING EXOTIC PLANTS INDOORS

bright conditions should not be given if the plants have been used to shade for some time.

Plenty of water—except just after potting seedlings or planting in the baskets—should be given at all times, together with generous overhead spraying and damping down. In pipe-heated houses, water thrown on to the hot pipes so that it vaporizes will be found very growth-promoting.

The size of the pitchers varies greatly according to species—from 3 inches in *N. gracilis* to 7 inches in *N. rafflesiana*—but the size can sometimes be increased by stopping the plants after about five or six leaves have formed. Where space is limited this may be a necessity, because the plants often reach a considerable height. *N. khasiana* grows to a fantastic length if left uncontrolled. Not all the leaves will form pitchers at their tips. Some merely develop tendrils with which the plant climbs, and others remain as or-

Plate 18. Stages in the formation of a Nepenthes pitcher: (A) the pitcher begins at the end of a tendril, which forms an extension of a leaf; (B) the pitcher takes shape; (C) the pitcher is fully mature.

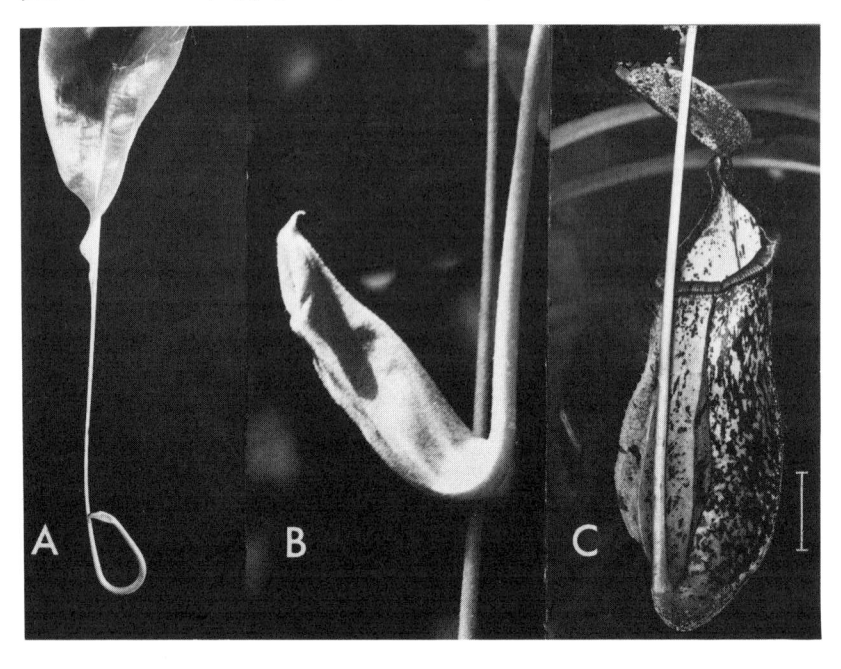

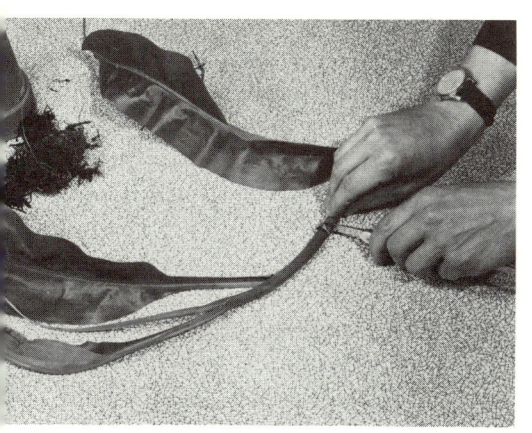

Touch-Sensitive, Motile, and Carnivorous Plants 73

Plates 19 and 20. Propagating Nepenthes: *left*, a cutting is made just below a leaf node in the normal manner; *right*, it is then inserted into a flowerpot as shown, so that the cut end reaches about the middle of the pot and is wedged in position with moss. The whole is then placed in a humid propagator at about 90° F.

dinary leaves. It is most interesting to follow the development of a fully grown pitcher from the very early stages. The lid usually remains tightly closed until the pitcher is at a sufficient stage of advancement to receive its first meal (Plate 18).

The best way to start with nepenthes is to acquire small plants during summer. They can also be grown from seed sown in a mixture of peat and chopped sphagnum moss kept at a temperature of about 80° F., as already described. But when you have growing plants, it is not easy to propagate them. Cuttings can be taken in the normal way, but they are difficult to root and usually rot. A special technique of air-rooting is employed (Plates 19 and 20). To perform this technique, a side shoot is cut from the plant and reduced to three or four leaves, the final cut being just below a pair of leaf nodes as with ordinary cuttings. The stem is then inserted through the drainage hole of an inverted flowerpot and wedged in position with sphagnum moss so that the end of the cut stem is suspended in air at about the center of the pot. The whole is then placed in a propagating case at about 90° F. with bottom heat and kept thoroughly humid. When the roots have formed, the pot may be broken away with a pair of pliers so as not to damage the roots, or in some cases it may be possible to draw the leaves down through the drainage hole if the orifice is large enough. Another technique that can be tried is air-layering. To do this, a pair of leaves are removed from a side shoot, a wad of sphagnum moss is wound around the stem at the point of removal, and afterwards covered with plastic wrap which is tied above and below the wad of moss. When roots can be seen through the plastic wrap, the shoot is severed just below the rooting area and potted.

Although most of the pitcher plants are normally grown in hanging baskets because of their epiphytic preferences, some can be successfully grown in pots.

The Sarraceniaceae

In this family can also be found some very attractive pitcher plants, although in this case the pitchers are usually more funnel-shaped or tubular (Plate 22). The three genera are the monotypic Darlingtonia of California, Heliamphora (which occurs in British Guiana and Venezuela), and the North American Sarracenia. The Sarraceniaceae differ from other carnivorous plants because the liquid at the bottom of their pitchers appears to contain no proteolytic enzyme, and the digestion is carried out by bacterial action.

Darlingtonia should present few cultural difficulties. It can be grown in a soil mix consisting of peat, sharp sand, sphagnum moss, and charcoal, contained in a half-pot stood in an inch or so of water. A bell-jar cover is not always necessary. Potting is best done during March when the plants are not in vigorous growth. Seed, which should be fairly fresh, should be sown on the surface of sphagnum moss, as previously described, and covered with glass. Propagation can be effected from side shoots. Cool shady conditions are desirable at all stages of growth.

Touch-Sensitive, Motile, and Carnivorous Plants 75

The pitchers of *Darlingtonia californica* (Plate 21) have a remarkable resemblance to a rearing snake and are slightly translucent. A nectar-like substance, which attracts insects, is exuded in the upper interior of the hood, but the creatures are unable to escape because of numerous downward-pointing hairs.

Heliamphora has five species, but only *H. nutans* is frequently seen. It is very similar to sarracenia in appearance and culture but needs warmer conditions.

Sarracenia is best treated as half-hardy. The pitchers are shaped like long trumpets, and the plant is sometimes called Trumpet Leaf. Most strange-looking flowers are produced on long stems. The style of the flower is so highly developed that it extends above the ovary to form an umbrella-like structure. The stigmatic surfaces are located at the five tips of the "umbrella," and the stamens are underneath.

Plates 21 and 22. Pitcher plants: *left*, the snake-like pitchers of *Darlingtonia californica* and the flower; *right*, the trumpet-shaped pitchers of Sarracenia.

Culture is very similar to that described for Darlingtonia, but if grown from seed it is essential that fresh seed should be sown; otherwise it is not likely to be viable. Sarracenias like much humidity, and a bell jar, slightly raised for ventilation, may be necessary if a greenhouse is not available.

Experimenting with Carnivorous Plants

All of the carnivorous plants can be fed via their traps in order to demonstrate their digestive action. However, it is important that only tiny fragments of food should be given at any one time. Suitable materials are high protein foods such as lean meat and boiled egg-white; cheese is less suitable.

Venus's Flytrap will completely liquefy egg white in about 30 hours. Pitcher plants take about 8 hours if the pitchers are mature. After pitchers have been in action for some time, they usually become colonized by bacteria, which helps in the digestion.

Unlike the human stomach, which contains the mineral acid hydrochloric acid, pitchers contain organic acids (such as formic acid) to aid digestion. It should be understood that the acid cannot have any effect unless the enzymes are present; the acid is too dilute to have any ordinary corrosive effect. Considerable dilution of the liquid owing to careless watering will spoil the digestive action. On the other hand, continually emptying a pitcher of its digestive fluid causes it to wither and die. An atmosphere that is too dry has the same result.

If pieces of food that are too large are given to any of the carnivorous plants, bacterial decay of the food sets in, and this may cause rotting of surrounding plant tissue. The clams of Venus's Flytrap wither and drop off, but the rest of the plant is not likely to suffer.

Recent investigation of the fluid in pitcher plants seems to indicate that a wetting agent is also present, the purpose of which is to wet and drown the prey more effectively, to facilitate the ensuing chemical reactions. Many insects and similar creatures are coated with a protective film of oil or wax-like material which tends to repel water, and the pitcher plants have evolved to deal with such a situation.

Plate 23. A very large specimen of the Staghorn Fern.

4

STRANGE OR UNUSUAL PLANTS

THE vegetable kingdom—like all other branches of Nature—is full of wonders if one takes the trouble to look for them. From so many possibilities it is difficult to decide which to select. In this chapter I have grouped together details of a number of plants that cannot be classified with the specific types described under other chapter headings, but are of interest because of their appearance, habits, or properties.

Some readers are bound to find what they consider serious omissions, but I must point out that my selection has been confined to plants with which I am well familiar, to plants that are not too difficult to obtain, and with a few exceptions to plants that I think most people will be able to grow without too much trouble.

In many cases the plants can be grown indoors on a windowsill or on an apartment balcony. But I have included one or two difficult subjects which are interesting for this very reason and offer a challenge to the more experienced gardener.

Aristolochia. Aristolochiaceae

Aristolochia is a fairly large genus many species of

which have been used in medicine in the treatment of snake bite, syphilis, rheumatism, and indigestion, and as abortifacients and emmenagogues. It is from the latter use in regulating menstruation that the family and genus derive their name, which means "best parturition". In spite of their widespread employment in medicine, their value is doubtful, and there are only two species, *A indica* and *A. reticulata*, still very occasionally used in dyspepsia medicines today.

Aristolochias are varied in habit and usually come from warm climates. The flowers are often extraordinary in shape and sometimes resemble the pitchers of nepenthes (see page 72). The structure of the flower is so designed that visiting insects secure pollination (Fig. 15), and often a rather unpleasant odor is emitted that serves to attract flies.

We will consider here only the species *Aristolochia elegans*, which is very decorative and bears remarkable flowers. Although this is often described as being a warm greenhouse species (since it is indigenous to Brazil), I have grown it quite successfully in a greenhouse with a minimum winter temperature of 45° F. Once established it is a vigorous but pleasing climber that can be trained easily and grown in a pot. It must have something to climb up, and wires are best because it climbs by twisting of the stem rather in the manner of convolvulus.

Seed is usually obtainable, but I must admit that I have had great difficulty with germination. This may have been because the seed was not sufficiently fresh. In view of the poor germination I prefer to sow the seeds on pads of cotton wool as described in Chapter 5, page 111, with a germination temperature of about 65° F. Germination is erratic, and as soon as a seed is seen to begin it should be immediately transferred to a small pot of a medium soil mix and lightly covered with some fine peat. The seedlings are best accommodated in a warm propagating case at about 60° F. until well established. If seed is sown in spring, fair-sized plants will be obtained by the end of the year. Little growth is made in winter,

Strange or Unusual Plants 81

when the plants should be very sparingly watered; but the following year rapid growth is made, and they will require potting into 5-inch pots and perhaps later into 7-inch pots. They will also need to be provided with something to climb up at this stage. Flowering may occur in the second year during late summer or early autumn, but should be certain the third year, when the vine should be in its permanent position. In summer plenty of water should be applied and an occasional dose of liquid food. Cuttings will usually root readily in a warm propagating case.

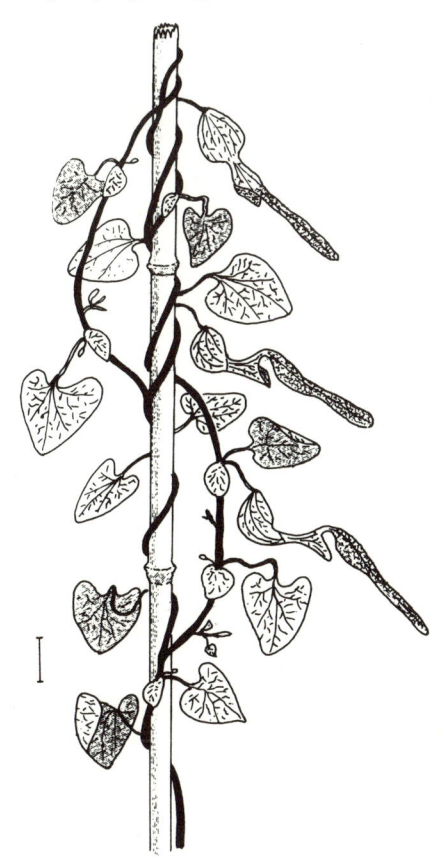

Fig. 15. Aristolochias have pitcher-like flowers resembling those of Nepenthes. Some species are called Dutchman's Pipe.

Plate 24. Young Bromeliads to be planted in a bottle garden: *left to right*, *Vriesia splendens, Cryptanthus bivittatus, Aregelia carolinae.*

The flowers are most unusual in appearance but delightful and freely produced. They are about 2 inches long and tubular, the stem end being inflated. The coloring is a mixture of cream, purple, and brown, and they are attractively veined and mottled.

Bromeliads (The Pineapple Family) Bromeliaceae

Bromeliad is the name given to members of the Bromeliaceae, (Plate 24), better known as the pineapple family. Most people enjoy eating the delicious fruits of *Ananas comosus*, which is nutritious and rich in vitamin C, but probably few gardeners have thought of growing it. Excellent pineapples can be grown under glass, but it is not possible unless a high temperature can be maintained.

Ideally a minimum winter temperature of 65° F. is required for pineapples, but they will resist much lower temperature if they are kept drier. A medium soil mix is suitable for pineapples. In summer plenty of water should be given and the atmosphere kept as humid as possible.

The spiky top of the ordinary pineapple can sometimes be rooted if the fruit is not too old. The top is merely cut off with a sharp knife, the first lower leaves removed, and the remainder planted in a small pot containing a light soil mix. It should then be put into a propagating case with a high temperature and moist atmosphere, but the soil should be kept only slightly moist. During a long, warm summer it is sometimes possible to root them in a greenhouse without any extra heat, but they will not survive the winter without warmth.

Other bromeliads differ widely in their temperature requirements and ease of culture, but many grow naturally in the mountains of South America and are used to wide temperature fluctuations; these make excellent house plants. Species from warm parts of Central America are best suited to greenhouse culture.

Bromeliads may be epiphytic (meaning that they may grow above ground rooted to mossy tree trunks or vines), or terrestrial and rooted in the ground, as with most ordinary plants. Most of the latter type have barbed leaves (like pineapple tops), whereas the epiphytes usually have smooth-edged leaves. The leaves are rosette- or star-shaped and often bear extremely striking and attractive markings. In many cases there is a cup-shaped hollow at the center of the rosette, which contains water. It is most important when growing these plants that the cup should be kept filled with water. This little reservoir supplies the plant's requirements and renders it less dependent on the roots. It is believed that the water cup also acts in a similar way as in the carnivorous plants by drowning insects and collecting plant debris, the rotting of which makes available nitrogenous materials absorbed by the plant. The fact that many bromeliads also contain the proteolytic enzyme bromelian is especially suggestive. In cultivation, diluted fertilizer can be given via the water cup with advantage, but sometimes it is advisable to

84 GROWING EXOTIC PLANTS INDOORS

wash out the cup from time to time to prevent the possibility of offensive odors arising should the water become foul.

It is interesting that few of the showy-leaved bromeliads produce equally spectacular flowers; conversely, many of those with rather dull-looking leaves compensate by displaying blooms of an extraordinary and colorful kind. The flowers of some species are ephemeral, but the bracts (which are usually brightly colored) can retain their attractiveness for months.

The rosette of a bromeliad flowers only once, but it produces new young plants from around the base. These should be removed and potted, whereupon they will flower usually in about one to two years.

Various mixtures of peat, leaf mold, sharp sand, and charcoal can be used for bromeliads. Large pots are unnecessary—about 4-5 inches is the maximum size needed—and frequent repotting should be avoided.

If germinating and greenhouse facilities are available, seed can be sown; but this is a slow way of obtaining plants, and it may take several years before flowers can be expected. An easier way is to purchase small plants, usually propagated from side shoots, from the various specialist nurseries during spring. Most bromeliads prefer slight shade during summer and plenty of light in winter. In general, if the temperature is near the minimum required in winter, it is best to keep the plants rather dry; but in summer, watering can be liberal, and a moist atmosphere is most beneficial. It is advisable in winter not to let the temperature fall much below 45° F., and, if possible, it should be a bit higher.

Some easy bromeliads especially suited to the beginner are listed below:

Aechmea rhodocyanea. Prefers light position; good leaf markings, exotic flowers and bracts. When flowers shrivel, promptly remove them from the bracts with forceps.

Bilbergia nutans. Slight shade; bears strange pendant flowers, leaves not rosettes.

Strange or Unusual Plants 85

Cryptanthus bivittatus (plate 24). Chameleon Plant, see below.

Cryptanthus zonatus. Very attractive markings; keep water off the leaves, good for warm, dry rooms.

Neoregelia carolinae tricolor. Good foliage, flowers insignificant and soon die—promptly remove.

Vriesa splendens (Plate 24). Very easy indoors, good for shady corners, nicely colored leaves.

Of these, *Cryptanthus bivittatus roseus pictus* is an outstanding curiosity, and is better known by the shorter name of Chameleon Plant. It earned this name through its ability to vary its color according to the amount of light received. The arrangement of the leaves is star-shaped, and each leaf, in the shade, is pale green with a darker stripe running down the center. If moved to a sunny position, the leaf color changes to pink and maroon. If removed back to the shade, it reverts to its original two-tone green.

An interesting recent discovery is that if bromeliads show reluctance to flower under cultivation they can be induced to do so by treatment with ethylene, a gas evolved from ripe apples. The bromeliad and a ripe apple are sealed in a plastic bag for several days. After such treatment, many bromeliads are said to flower within about six months.

Calonyction (Moonflower). Convolvulaceae

The convolvulus family is well known to all gardeners, either in the form of the beautiful-flowered Morning Glory *(Pharbitis tricolor)* or as the troublesome Bindweed *(Convolvulus arrensis).* The genus Calonyction is not as commonly encountered, since it is really a native of the tropics. There are only three species, and all of them flower at night—hence the genus name, which means "beautiful night." Of these species, *Calonyction aculeatum* (Plate 25) is the most readily available, and it does indeed live up to its common name of Moonflower. Like most of the Convolvulaceae, the buds first take the shape of long spikes. These

Plate 25. The large, fragrant Moonflower.

open at dusk to form enormous pure white flowers often exceeding 5 inches across. A rose-pink form is also available. Their fragrance is intensely powerful and lily-like, and since the blooms are borne on short stems, they can be cut for indoor decoration.

The plant can best be appreciated if grown in a lean-to greenhouse or a conservatory that is part of a house. It can then be trained up the wall and perhaps down the roof, where its magnificent scented blossom will bring much pleasure during the evenings of July and August. With the coming of dawn the flowers close or fade, and during the day new buds prepare themselves for opening at dusk.

It is very convenient of the Convolvulaceae to provide us with two complementary plants like Morning Glory and the Moonflower, because grown together their beauty can be described as providing "day and night service."

Plate 26. The Glory Pea is difficult to raise, but the grower is rewarded with spectacular flowers in brilliant scarlet and shiny black.

The Moonflower is perennial and easily raised from seed. The seed should be soaked overnight and can be sown in small pots of peat and perlite. If sown in early spring, the plant will reach a considerable length and flower well the first year. Eventually it grows to about 10-12 feet. It is quite happy in pots, and in a conservatory or sun room three plants can be put in a 7-inch pot and trained up whatever happens to be convenient. Early sowings will need a warm propagating case, and in order for it to survive the winter a minimum temperature of about 45° F. is desirable. The Moonflower flowers well in either slight shade or full light. Although it is not fussy, the roots should not be allowed to become too dry.

Clianthus (Glory Pea). Leguminosae

The most commonly seen clianthus is *C. puniceus*, often called New Zealand Lobster Claw or Parrot's Bill; this is an evergreen shrub that is excellent for the cold greenhouse or conservatory, or for planting out in milder parts of the country. The flowers have a very strange appearance, from which the common name of the plant is derived, and are brilliantly colored red. There is also a white variety. This species is an excellent shrub, being most decroative and easy to grow; but a species of much greater interest is C. formosus, the Glory Pea (Plate 26)—it offers a challenge to those who consider themselves "green-fingered." The prize of success is the exceptionally bizarre vivid red and glistening black flower, but the plant is very difficult to grow on its own roots, and anyone who raises it to flowering size from seed has every right to feel proud and pleased.

Clianthus formosus is a native of the Australian desert land, where it rains rarely, but torrentially. After the rain the seeds germinate, but as the plants grow, conditions become drier. These conditions should offer some guidance to the plant's culture.

Seeds usually germinate without any difficulty whatsoever, but it does help to soak them about 24 hours before sowing. I cannot recommend any special soil mix because I have yet to find the ideal growing medium. I usually employ a mixture of loam, sphagnum moss, peat, sand, and charcoal, and I think that these are the sort of materials to experiment with. The seeds should be sown directly on the soil medium and thinned out, since they rarely survive transplanting. The great difficulty is in keeping the plant alive. Usually after an apparently good start, when the seedlings have reached about 5 inches or so, they gradually turn brown and die. If they are pulled out, the roots will be seen to be meager and shriveled. Should one of the seedlings appear to make satisfactory growth, it should on no account be disturbed. Try breaking away the bottom of the pot with pliers to allow free passage of the root, and wedge the pot on top of another pot or suitable container, such as a length of drain pipe, filled with a similar soil mix. In the plant's natural environment, the roots go straight down to a considerable depth, presumably to

Strange or Unusual Plants 89

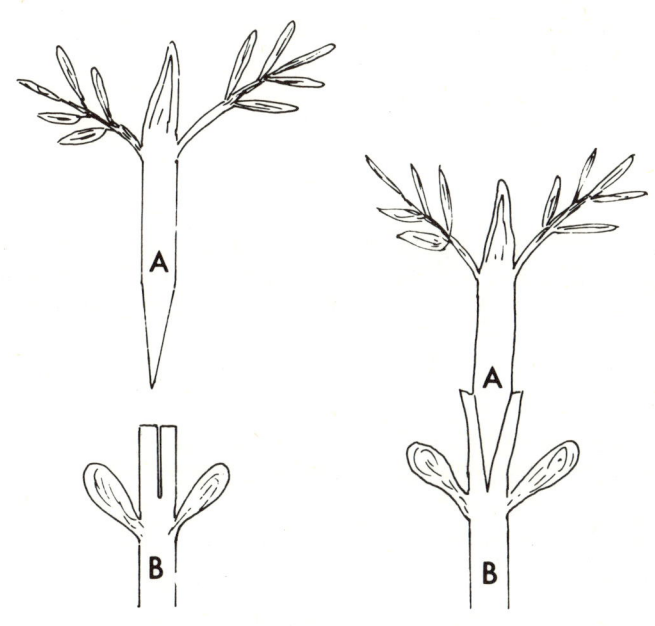

Fig. 16. Grafting Clianthus: (A) the shoot of a *Clianthus formosus* seedling is cut into a wedge with a razor blade and the root is discarded; (B) the wedge is inserted into a slit cut just above the cotyledon leaves of a *Colutea arborescens* seedling, the growing tip of the Colutea having been cut off and discarded.

reach a moisture level. However, in spite of this characteristic, some superb clianthus have been grown in hanging baskets.

The best way to attain more certain results is to graft the seedlings on to seedlings of *Colutea arborescens,* commonly called Bladder Senna. The latter plant will put up with all sorts of ill treatment and can be watered without fear of root rot. It is no use sowing the seeds of both plants at the same time, because colutea is much slower growing in the early stages and has thinner stems than clianthus; this makes it impossible to match up the stems when grafting. The work should commence early in spring with the sowing of colutea in a propagating case at about 60° F. using small pots. When the first true leaves are being formed above the cotyledons of the colutea, the clianthus can be sown in the light seed medium, since the roots are discarded. To be sure of matching the stem sizes it is best to carry out the sowings in batches at weekly intervals so that seedlings at various growth stages are available. The grafting can be done as illustrated in Fig. 16, the clianthus seedlings being attached in a slit made in the stem of the colutea just between the cotyledons. The graft can be held with a piece of soft knitting wool. After the operation the plants should be placed in a warm propagating case and the atmosphere kept humid until the union is effected, but if the grafting is done during summer, a bell-jar cover may be sufficient. The grafting when one is dealing with such small seedlings is a delicate procedure, and it may take a little practice before satisfactory results are obtained. Success will be achieved only if the operation is tackled with confidence and one is prepared not to be discouraged by failure at first. Once the graft has taken—which will be obvious by a slight swelling at the union and by continued top growth—the plant can be potted as required in ordinary soil mixes to which a little extra sand has been added to ensure perfect drainage. If the graft has not taken, the clianthus top will merely wither and die off. Only *seedlings* of colutea are suitable for grafting, because as they mature they become woody-stemmed, and the stems have hollow centers.

Since *Clianthus formosus* is a trailing plant, it can be allowed to tumble from a hanging basket, trail along a greenhouse border, or be trained up some kind of support. It should be given plenty of light and air and not too much humidity.

In winter *C. formosus* will survive temperatures down to nearly freezing provided it is kept fairly dry.

Davallia Mariesii (Japanese Fern Balls). Polypodiaceae

Various nurserymen have recently listed Japanese Fern Balls as a curiosity in their catalogues. The balls consist of rhizomes of the very attractive dwarf Japanese fern, *Davallia mariesii*, twisted around a core of sphagnum moss and peat and held in position with galvanized iron or copper wire. A loop is attached so that the ball can be hung (Plate 27).

Plate 27. A Japanese Fern Ball beginning to sprout.

There is nothing especially strange or unusual about *D. mariesii*. The novelty lies in that the prepared balls can be dried off during winter and forgotten about until spring. They are then taken from the odd drawer or cupboard, thoroughly soaked with water, and hung up in a shady place. After a short period, the balls sprout dainty fronds until their surface is absolutely covered. It is quite happy as an indoor plant provided that the ball is kept moist by periodic soaking or spraying. I find that ordinary hard tap water has no deleterious effect.

A rather unexpected property of these balls is that they seem to carry on for years without any need for fertilizer or changing of the core. Ideally a temperature of about 50-60° F. is best, and it is essential that they do not receive direct sunlight, or the fronds will shrivel and turn brown.

Lophophora Williamsii (Mescal Button)

In the class of plants known as succulents can be found many curiosities: lithops, or "living stones," for example, which are succulents that appear to be quite lifeless pebbles but produce large, daisy-like, showy flowers. The succulents are fairly well documented in the many specialist books devoted to them, but I have singled out one that is especially fascinating—not so much on account of its appearance, but because of its properties and history. It is *Lophophora williamsii*, better known as the Mescal Button (Plate 28).

The natural habitat of the mescal cactus is northern Mexico, Chihuahua, Zacateus, and parts of Texas. In Mexico a distilled intoxicant drink is prepared from the agave and given the name of mescal, thus sometimes leading to confusion with peyote, a similar liquor prepared from the Mescal Button.

Most of the cactus is below ground in the form of a large tap-root structure. From this arises the "button," which is dotted at intervals with tufts of whitish hair but bears no cactus-like spines or bristles. From the center emerge a succession of pinkish flowers followed by pinkish fruits. The flowers last only a day and do not fully open unless the surroundings are warm.

Mescal Buttons have a very ancient history and were well known to the Aztecs, who called them "sacred mushrooms" and employed them in religious ceremonies, but the cactus was little investigated until Lemair placed it in the genus Echinocactus in 1845. Lewin, in 1886, named it Anhalonium, and Coulter has since made it the type of a new genus Lophophora; it still retains this name.

When eaten or prepared as a drink, the Mescal Button has a very peculiar physiological and psychological action, the most startling effects being extremely vivid and colorful

Strange or Unusual Plants 93

Plate 28. The Mescal Cactus.

hallucinations. Brilliant colored patterns, flashing lights, and exotic visions are experienced. These are accompanied by the impression of being capable of profound thought, a general feeling of well-being, and an almost spiritual sensation of separation from the material world. It can readily be appreciated why the Mescal Button has been valued as an aid to religious ceremony: its use could have had a very great influence on primitive peoples.

The hallucinatory properties of mescal were utilized by the Kiowa Indians of the Rio Grande, who made the eating of the buttons by the congregation a part of religious rituals. It was also eaten before battles because it banished all fear, gave apparent strength, and produced the effect of a mental tranquilizer and energy "pep pill" combined. Even as late as 1918 slices of Mescal Button were used to replace the bread and wine at communion service in a Peyote church founded in

Mexico. No doubt the resulting colorful hallucinations and other effects were attributed to a divine origin.

If eaten in large quantities, mescal fixes the limbs in strange, grotesque positions where they remain for a considerable time. This weird behavior must have greatly enhanced the psychological value of mescal at religious meetings.

A number of present-day psychological research workers—as well as a few people who are always seeking new sensations—have eaten mescal to test its effects. They claim that an accurate description of the result is impossible because the sensations produced are outside normal human experience. Further information can be found in *The Doors of Perception* by Aldous L. Huxley, which records his experiences after taking mescalin. All the same, I would not advise eating the cactus, since the administration of such powerful vegetable drugs should be carried out only under medical supervision. The hallucinatory properties, mainly due to a substance called mescalin, are said to resemble those produced by certain seeds of the Convolvulaceae which contain a similar drug; although garden varieties—including Morning Glory—are harmless.

As a decorative plant the Mescal Button is not unattractive, and it is an excellent addition to any cactus collection. Its cultural requirements are similar to mammillaria. It requires plenty of sunshine and has a tendency to shrivel during winter, when water should be withheld. In spring, on gradually commencing watering, it swells and resumes growth.

Musa (banana). Musaceae

Owing to its high temperature requirements, rapid growth, and considerable size, the ordinary fruiting banana is rarely grown other than in the large greenhouses of botanic gardens. Given the right conditions, however, it is easy to cultivate and grows with incredible speed. Most fruit-forming varieties do not form seed but are readily propa-

Strange or Unusual Plants 95

Plate 29. The Abyssinian Banana, *Musa ensete*.

gated from suckers; these will grow to about 15-20 feet in a matter of months and yield a fine stalk of bananas. The merit of the fruit as a nutritious food needs no comment; but very recently the dried unripe pulp has been found to have a pronounced inhibiting effect on the development of duodenal ulcers in rats, and it remains to be seen whether this discovery can be put to use in the treatment of man.

Although the edible banana is not a practical proposition for the ordinary gardener, there is one species that can be fairly easily grown. It is my favorite foliage plant, and one that I really enjoy growing—the Abyssinian banana, *Musa ensete* (Plate 29). The magnificent huge leaves and stately tropical appearance of this plant never fail to arouse attention and admiration. Most people ask to be informed of its identity and greet the reply with awe or disbelief.

Musa ensete can be grown from seed, which is usually readily available—but it must be reasonably fresh, since it quickly loses its viability after one or two years. The seed is very large and bean-like, and I find that germination is often erratic and only about 40 percent. The possibility of only about four successes out of ten seeds does not usually matter, because even two plants will eventually fill the average small greenhouse. The seed should be soaked for about 24 hours before sowing and then shallowly immersed in a pan of moist peat contained in a propagating case at about 70° F. Some seeds may germinate in less than a month and others may take longer. As soon as a seed begins to sprout, it should be immediately transferred to a small pot of peat and perlite and kept in a warm propagating case. The best time to sow is in late spring when the warmer weather begins, but once growth starts, it continues briskly and frequent repotting will be necessary. By early autumn a 7-inch pot will be needed, and the plants will have reached about 4-5 feet in height and bear enormous leaves. This growth rate can be achieved with normal summer temperatures in an unheated greenhouse or conservatory.

During a cold summer, when the temperature fluctuates widely, and also during the first year of growth, the lower leaves often have a tendency to turn brown. Over winter the plants can be kept in a greenhouse with a minimum temperature of about 45° F., but most of the leaves will probably die off at this temperature and should be carefully detached from the main stem with a sharp knife or razor blade. However, as soon as the temperature starts to rise in spring, growth again begins at a fantastic rate and the plants will require shifting to a 12-inch pot. By early June of the second year, they will have reached magnificent proportions, with nine or ten huge, pale green leaves; it is at this stage that their size can cause some problems.

Musa ensete is one of the most impressive plants for a large conservatory or sun porch, and anyone who has these facilities really must grow it. In very sheltered parts of the country it can be planted outdoors as a subtropical centerpiece; but outdoors in spring, summer, and autumn the enemy is not cold but wind. The gigantic leaves are very easily torn, and even a moderate gale will reduce them to tatters. Except in a very mild locality they will be killed in winter outdoors.

It is always sad to have to part with a beautiful foliage plant, but where space is limited it is usually best to discard the plants at the close of their second year and start again from seed.

The Abyssinian banana seems to grow well in partial shade or full sunlight. Plenty of water is needed during growth, but it should be kept only slightly moist during winter. Generous feeding should be provided during the growing period. It makes a good room plant for a very large room, especially where there is a capacious bay window.

This species does not produce edible fruit, but it finds use as a source of fiber. In its natural habitat it grows 20-30 feet in height, and its leaves can exceed about 15 feet in length.

Platycerium (Staghorn Fern). Polypodiaceae

This is a genus of extraordinary looking ferns very aptly called Staghorn ferns. The fact that these very odd ferns can be attached to and grown on a square of wood and fastened to a wall adds to the appropriateness of the common names. It is a pity that those people who go around aiding the destruction of the already dwindling natural fauna, in order merely to decorate their walls with horns, cannot be persuaded to substitute the less bloodthirsty pastime of platycerium growing.

Most of the platycerium ferns are not easy to cultivate; they are all epiphytic and need a warm and moist atmosphere. *Platycerium bifurcatum* (Plate 23) is an exception because it can be grown well at ordinary cool greenhouse temperatures, provided that the temperature does not fall below about 45-60° F. during winter. Unfortunately, a good specimen of this fern will be rather expensive. It is often listed in nurserymen's catalogues as *P. alcicorne*.

The cultural techniqe is rather different from other ferns. Since platyceriums are epiphytic they must be planted in a mixture of fibrous peat and sphagnum moss or in osmundine (a potting material made from the aerial roots of tree ferns and used in potting orchids). This mixture can either be fastened to pieces of bark or cork and suspended from the greenhouse ceiling, or it can be contained in hanging slatted baskets of the type used for epiphytic orchids. The most effective way of growing them, if space permits, is to obtain a piece of forked tree branch, thoroughly clean it to free it from any possible pests or fungi, and fasten the growing medium and platyceriums in the fork after fixing the branch upright. A position where there is plenty of light should be chosen, but in my opinion direct sunlight is best avoided. For fastening, it is most important to use a rust-proof or corrosion-proof wire (such as plastic-covered or copper wire); otherwise the wire might rust after repeated waterings and allow the fern to come loose from the base.

Watering requires special care. The base material must always be thoroughly soaked when water is given, which is best done with a coarse spray, but it must not be kept in a perpetually waterlogged condition. The growing medium should be allowed to dry sufficiently for the ferns to wilt—only very slightly—before water is again applied. Rain water or other soft water should be used.

Platycerium bifurcatum is probably best displayed on the wall of a lean-to greenhouse or conservatory in order to take full advantage of its strange stag's horn appearance. In the plant's natural habitat, the basal upright frond (which is sterile) collects plant debris into which the fern subsequently roots.

Sauromatum (Monarch of the East). Araceae.

The Araceae is well known for its curiosities—some grotesque and others beautiful in a rather weird way. One of the most spectacular is *Amorphophallus giganteus* which produces a fantastically large leaf and inflorescence and emits a fetid odor, but here we will consider something more within the scope of the ordinary gardener.

Sauromatum guttatum (Plate 30) is better known as Monarch of the East and is also sometimes known as *Arum cornutum*. When purchased *S. guttatum* is in the form of a flattened bulb, which is a tuber. This tuber should be placed on a little sand in a saucer to keep it upright and kept under observation. At this stage it requires no soil or water. After a time a shoot will appear from the center and subsequently will develop a very strange arum-like "flower" properly called an inflorescence. It has a long purple-spotted spathe that soon trails and shrivels, and sometimes a disagreeable smell is evolved that attracts flies. When this happens it is best to remove the plant outdoors if, as is usually the practice, it is being grown on an indoor windowsill. The flowers rarely last more than a day, but when they produce a revolting stench, it is just as well.

After flowering, the tubers should be potted in a 5-inch pot of peat and perlite, planting them about an inch or so deep. The soil mixture should be kept slightly moist, and before long the next spectacle, in the form of a large palm-like leaf on a stout spotted stem, will be produced. At this stage the plant makes a very attractive and exotic-looking foliage plant. The tubers usually become available in spring and flower soon after purchasing. The foliage is developed shortly after flowering and remains effective until autumn. When the foliage dies down, the corm can be removed from

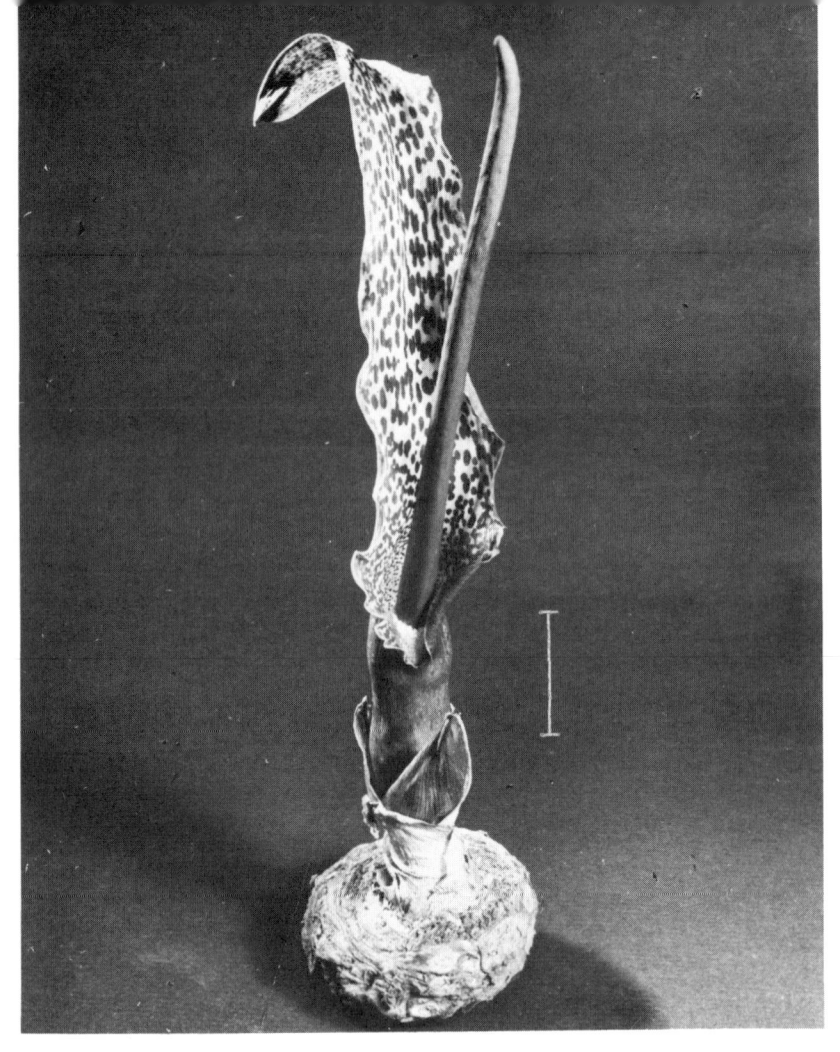

Plate 30. Monarch of the East, *Sauromatum guttatum,* flowers without soil or water.

the pot and stored until the following year. One corm also usually produces a large number of offsets, but it is not really worth growing these because the large flowering-size corms are very cheap. A good tuber should be about 4 inches across, but the larger they are, the more spectacular the results. Very small ones may not flower.

Strelitzia (Bird of Paradise Flower). Musaceae

The exotic Bird of Paradise Flower, *Strelitzia regina* (Plate 31), belongs to the banana family and never fails to

Strange or Unusual Plants 101

excite wonder and admiration. Contrary to popular belief, high temperatures are not required, and very large specimens can be seen in conservatories and temperate greenhouses, where they flower prolifically.

Strelitzia is remarkable in several ways, and although it is often described, little is written about its interesting pollination, which is an excellent example of ornithophily—pollination by birds. In South Africa, where the plant is indigenous, the flower is pollinated by a little Honey Bird *(Nectarina afra)* which has beautiful breast colorings of brilliant orange and blue similar to the Bird of Paradise Flower itself. The bird settles on a part of the flower shaped as a convenient landing perch and in doing so transfers some pollen from its breast (acquired during a visit to another flower) to the stigma of its present host. It then walks

Plate 31. In its natural home the Bird of Paradise flower is pollinated by a Honey Bird, which alights on the stigma (A) and moves along to obtain nectar from the reservoir (C). When the bird bends to drink, its breast touches the anthers (B), and pollen is transferred to be later deposited on the stigma of another flower. The flower has showy orange sepals (D).

along to a part of the flower where a dome-shaped petal covers a nectary. To reach the reservoir of nectar, it must lower its head and at the same time gather on its breast feathers pollen from the stamens, which are so situated that transfer cannot be avoided. Having partaken the delicious nectar, the bird flies off to another flower, and so the process of pollination is repeated. The name Bird of Paradise Flower has nothing to do with ornithophily and is derived from the exotic appearance of the very large flower.

Flowering-size plants of *S. regina* are rather expensive, but the price is dependent on the growth stage. Seeds are also comparatively highly priced. To grow strelitzia to flowering size from seed takes three to five years.

Seed must be reasonably fresh, or germination will be erratic and poor. The seeds are about the size of those of sweet pea but have a bright orange tuft of fibers. They should be sown in early spring just below the surface of fine moist peat or on a cotton wool pad (page 111), and placed in a propagating case at about 75-80° F. As soon as a seed germinates it should be transferred immediately with forceps to a small pot of light soil mix and left in the propagator. Growth is slow, and the extra warmth in the early stages will help the plants to become established. Strelitzias are monocotyledonous, and consequently, after germination and transference to pots, it may be some time before a leaf appears above the surface. In the meantime, root growth will be taking place. It is to avoid damaging the root that I prefer the surface sowing for initial germination. Surface sowing can be done under more sterile conditions, whereas if sowing is done directly in pots, the seeds often rot before germination commences (page 111). Surface sowing means that you can see at once whether the seed is viable, and after potting it requires no further disturbance until the roots are sufficiently well developed to need a larger pot. Germination will be aided by giving the seeds a good soaking for at least 48 hours before sowing.

After potting, the plants will make slow but steady growth. Root growth is usually greater than might be expected from the number and size of the leaves, but this is a good thing. The roots are large and fleshy and should not be allowed to become pot bound. A rather heavy soil mix with more than one half loam is an ideal growing medium, and a final pot size of about 8 inches is usually sufficient for flowering. If the plant can be grown in a greenhouse border, all the better.

There are a number of species of strelitzia all bearing similar shaped flowers, although the colors vary, but I think that *S. regina* is best from the point of view of both attractiveness and compactness. It grows to only about 3-4 feet in height, whereas other species can double this. Flowers usually appear in late winter, early spring, or summer and tend to be rather erratic. I have known the plant to bloom at the most unexpected times. For best results a winter minimum temperature of about 50° F. is desirable.

104 GROWING EXOTIC PLANTS INDOORS

Plate 32. Ornamental Pepper, *Piper ornatum,* is a handsome foliage plant that can be grown from seed.

5

GROWING PLANTS FROM SEED

IT is often written that to increase the likelihood of success in growing a plant it is essential to try to reproduce the climate of its native country, and on first consideration this seems sound advice. Unfortunately this recommendation must stem from the armchair horticultural expert, because anyone with even the smallest amount of experience and practical knowledge will be able to name many cases in which plants will thrive in conditions not at all like those of their native habitat.

What is sometimes useful is a knowledge of the native soil conditions, especially with regard to drainage and water requirements. Some plants are extremely fussy and need very specialized soils. Typical are many of our wild orchids, which are astonishingly localized to quite small areas. Any attempt to cultivate them elsewhere is usually doomed to failure. Conversely, some plants can be cultivated in conditions that exist nowhere outside the laboratory and can be grown perfectly well in nutrient aggregates and jellies.

Given an unusual plant, my advice is therefore to try to find out as much as possible about its native country by all means, but do not be discouraged by what you learn. Try growing it, however impossible it may be to reproduce the climate and its normal requirements. Plants often grow better in cultivation than they do in the wild.

To the gardener interested in unusual or lesser known plants, growing from seed is an important cultural technique, as the great majority of unusual plants are available only in this form. To be able to grow plants from seed is useful to all gardeners, and it is the best and cheapest way to raise strong plants. One knows the cultural history of the plants, and they are not set back or damaged like those that have to suffer shipping adventures.

In view of the advantages of growing one's own plants from seed, it is surprising that so few amateur gardeners know very much about seed and its germination, and I have been astonished at the careless and slapdash sowing methods that are frequently adopted. Many gardening books and periodicals are also vague about seed sowing and germination, and it is remarkable that very elementary items of information that may be essential to the complete success or failure of germination are frequently omitted. All gardeners—and, let it be noted, seedsmen and wholesalers—should be thoroughly acquainted with the requirements of germination and storage of seeds. A number of dealers are guilty of selling seeds that are definitely not viable through age or through genetic, harvesting, or storage faults. I have found this to be so by carrying out independent viability tests using controls known to be reliable, and laboratory techniques involving microscopic examination of sections of the seed after staining by chemical methods (such as tetrazolium salt). Some examples of seeds that I have found to be supplied occasionally in a nonviable condition or giving very poor germination are: *Coffea arabica, Aralia elegantissima, Moluccella laevis,* Sarracenia and Darlingtonia species, Bertolonia species, *Isolepis gracilis (Scirpus cernuus), Ficus elastica,* Fuchsia, *Carica papaya, Aristolochia elegans,* Strelitzia species, palms, and *Begonia rex.* Most of these soon lose their viability on storage. If one is certain that the seeds are nonviable, one is justified in complaining, but unfortunately amatuer gardeners are more usually responsible for seed failure. I have received many samples of seeds claimed by gardeners to be useless, only to find on testing that there is nothing wrong with them. Some seed firms now claim to have their own testing laboratories.

Viability of Seeds

The viability of seeds is affected by a number of conditions, including their genetic history, the ripening process, their age, exposure to light, and storage conditions.

Hybridization can result in a loss of fertility and the production of nonviable seeds; this can sometimes prove a setback during the development of new varieties, although there are occasionally ingenious methods of crossing that can be used to overcome such a possibility.

Many seeds need to be ripened on the plant for optimum viability, and these are often those types that are produced by plants with special arrangements for distribution of seed. However, complete ripening on the plant is not always essential, and there are seeds that normally ripen after they have been shed; these are known as after-ripening seeds.

Age has an important influence on viability. There is no truth in the peculiar stories about seeds recovered from Egyptian tombs germinating after being incarcerated for many thousands of years. Investigation has shown that any germination has been due to contamination with fresh seeds after collection. Nevertheless, it is known with certainty that the Indian Lotus, *Nelumbo nucifera,* will retain viability for at least two hundred years and possibly for as long as a thousand years. Indian Lotus seeds known to be within this age have been dug out of mud where they have been deeply buried, and found to germinate perfectly well.

Sometimes viability is very short indeed and may in certain cases last only a few hours or days. In general, the seeds of cultivated plants tend to lose their viability more quickly than the seeds of wild plants. Many weed seeds, for example, will remain dormant for years if buried during digging, but will quickly germinate if brought to the surface again during some future gardening operation.

Storage of Seeds

Even seeds that are perfectly ripened and viable can soon be rendered completely nonviable by incorrect storage. A great many seeds are prone to attack by various fungi. These fungi are in general more likely to gain a hold if the seeds are stored in damp conditions. There are also, of course, the exceptions when thorough drying causes loss of viability. When seeds in packets are received from the dealer, they should be sown as soon as possible and not left in a damp place such as a greenhouse. If they must be kept for a time, they should be stored in a cool, airy room.

Seeds are often unexpectedly resistant to very low temperatures and have even been cooled to the temperature of liquid air, —310° F., without any ill effect. In fact some seeds are unable to germinate until they have been exposed to frost for a time; such treatment is known as stratification. Seeds of alpines, trees, and shrubs often need stratification.

High temperatures are likely to damage seeds. A few can withstand temperatures up to about 195° F., but in general about 175° F. will kill seeds or greatly reduce germination if maintained for about 10 minutes. This fact is made use of in the partial sterilization of soil mixes for seed sowing and potting. Weed seeds are destroyed as well as many pests and disease organisms.

Germination of Seeds

The important influence of light on the germination of many seeds is little known by the ordinary gardener, and it is interesting to conjecture how often failures may have resulted from this ignorance. The general assumption seems to be that all seeds need covering with soil, and this is very often carried to the extreme—which is a bad thing, for other reasons given later.

It is true that some seeds will germinate only in the dark—for example, cinerarias, begonias, coleus, and impatiens. However, some will germinate only in the light or after they have been exposed to light for a certain time. Others are completely indifferent. There are also seeds that are so particular that if they are exposed to light for a prolonged period they will refuse to germinate at all, although such seeds can often be made viable once again by treating with gibberellic acid.

Various other substances can also have a marked effect on the germination of seeds that normally need light to instigate viability; for example, such seeds may germinate perfectly well in the dark if they are first soaked in a solution of potassium nitrate (0.2 percent) or thiourea (0.5-3 percent). Thiourea treatment is also known to render stratification unnecessary in some cases. Exactly how these substances affect the biochemistry of the seed and bring about such changes is still very obscure.

Essential Germination Requirements

Seeds of any kind will fail to germinate unless they are maintained at a suitable temperature and are able to absorb oxygen and a little carbon dioxide together with moisture.

Temperature requirements vary greatly, but generally a temperature of about 60° F. is a good average to try first of all. Some may germinate well below 45° F. and most tropical plant seeds such as palms may require about 80° F. In certain cases a fluctuating temperature gives better germination, with the temperature falling at night. If the temperature is insufficient, there is risk of rotting, since the lower the temperature the longer germination will take. If the temperature is too low, the seeds will not germinate at all. Excessively high temperatures may kill the seed, or induce such rapid germination and subsequent growth that the seedlings become etiolated and useless.

It is not generally known that seeds undergo respiration and require oxygen and a little carbon dioxide (CO_2) in order to germinate. In an excess of carbon dioxide seeds remain dormant, and the lack of oxygen and predominance of CO_2 is believed to be largely responsible for the dormancy of seeds when they are buried deeply in the soil. During germination chemical processes take place within the seed that are the reverse of photosynthesis. For this reason seeds should never be sown deeply, and very often they need not be covered with soil, especially if the seeds are very minute. Waterlogged soils will also prevent the respiration of seeds. Although water is essential to germination, it should be present as moisture and not as wetness.

Some seeds can be helped to germinate if a tiny piece of the outer coating is peeled away—a process called scarifying. This procedure aids the penetration of water and air. Certain seeds will germinate better if they are first soaked by immersion in water for 12 hours or so, to swell and weaken the outer shell, and it is sometimes easier to peel the seeds after soaking them. These techniques should be well known to gardeners; sweet pea is a typical example that often receives such treatment.

Practical Sowing and Germinating Techniques

Soil Mixes for Germination

The best control over germination and the growth of seedlings in the early stages can be exercised when they are provided with a specially prepared, partially sterilized soil mix and given the protection of glass, such as a frame or small greenhouse with some means of artificially maintaining an optimum temperature. Many good commercial soil mixtures are available. Half peat and half perlite with a little sand added is commonly used.

Most commercial mixes contain only sufficient fertilizer for the seed's immediate requirements on germination and for its development little further than the cotyledon stage. Pricking out must therefore always be prompt. Early pricking out prevents damage to the root system, which would be more easily disturbed in the advanced state and cause a check to growth. It is especially important to prick out early those seedlings that are deep rooting; a well-known example is zinnia. Monocotyledonous seeds also need more prompt attention that dicotyledons. Large seeds can usually be sown directly in small pots.

Germination without Soil

In many cases, when one is in the possession of only a few rare seeds they can be germinated on moist cotton wool or blotting-paper pads. This method has the advantage that the conditions of germination can be almost or completely sterile—depending on the amount of care taken—and it is easier to experiment with different temperature conditions and exposures to light. The method is also very good for seeds that take a long time to germinate, as there is much less risk of their rotting through attack by fungi and bacteria. It is often used for testing the viability of seeds.

The pads of cotton wool or blotting paper must be placed in a container that can be closed to prevent the loss of moisture but which is sufficiently large to contain sufficient air for germination requirements and allow the formation of cotyledon leaves. A small glass dish is useful or a small Pyrex ovenware dish either fitted with a lid or covered with a sheet of glass. The pads are wetted with water so as to absorb the maximum amount of moisture without leaving an excess. The seeds are then placed on the top of the pad.

If it is desired to carry out the germination in sterile conditions, the dishes with the pads and lids in position must be sterilized in an oven at 320° F. for about 2 hours, and freshly boiled and cooled water must be used to moisten the pads. The seeds themselves may carry disease organisms on their surface and can be sterilized by immersion for a few minutes in a saturated solution of calcium hypochlorite (bleaching powder) and then rinsed thoroughly in water that has been boiled and cooled. Few seeds are damaged by this technique, and it is, in fact, used to sterilize orchid seeds before germinating—by the sterile nutrient jelly process. Most amateurs will probably fail to get their germinating dishes, pads, and seeds absolutely sterile, but they will be able to reduce the likelihood of attack by disease organisms considerably.

It should be realized that seeds germinated on pads are entirely dependent on the nutrients in the seed itself. A constant watch must be kept, and as soon as germination is seen to be taking place, the seeds should be individually transferred to a potting mix with the aid of finely pointed tweezers. The transplanted seedlings must then be maintained at a similar temperature until they have become established.

Seed Dressings

Another way to prevent rotting of seeds if they are of a type that takes a long time to germinate is to coat them with one of the modern seed dressings, of which there are several on the market. This is done by tipping a small quantity of the dressing, which is in the form of a fine powder, into the seed packet and shaking thoroughly. The seeds are then sown in the normal manner. This technique can be used for indoor germination, but it is especially useful for outdoor sowings, or indoor sowings when it is not possible to use sterilized soil mixes. However, there is a risk that certain uncommon plant seeds may be damaged by the dressing.

Incubators and Propagators

All gardeners interested in raising plants from seed must have a heated propagating case of some description. Although it is possible to use other means of heating, electricity is a tremendous advantage. Nowadays electricity is available to the majority of people, and since seed propagation needs only a little warmth, the amount of electricity used should be within the reach of most people's means. The types of propagator that can be employed vary enormously and range from an improvised tin box supported on bricks over an oil lamp and covered with glass, to an elaborate, thermo-

Growing Plants from Seed 113

statically controlled, automatically humidified electric propagator with adjustable temperature setting.

Excellent propagators can be made with heating cables, which can also be used in the garden for warming the soil and for heating garden frames. Raising plants from seed need not be enjoyed only by the fortunate owners of a greenhouse, conservatory, or sun porch, since a garden frame can be used with very good results and is a relatively inexpensive structure. Many people have to germinate and raise their seedlings with nothing better than an indoor windowsill.

Fig. 17 shows how an effective seed germinator can be improvised from a deep tin box with a little sand in the bottom and covered with a sheet of glass. The heat is provided by a small oil lamp or an electric bulb and by varying the distance of the tin from the heat source—or adjusting the lamp flame—quite a wide range of temperatures is possible. If electricity is used, a thermostat may be inserted in the tin to control the lamp heater. A couple of coats of enamel applied to the tin will prevent rust and give a pleasing professional finish. However, improvised electrical apparatus is always likely to be dangerous unless it is wired expertly with care given to proper grounding.

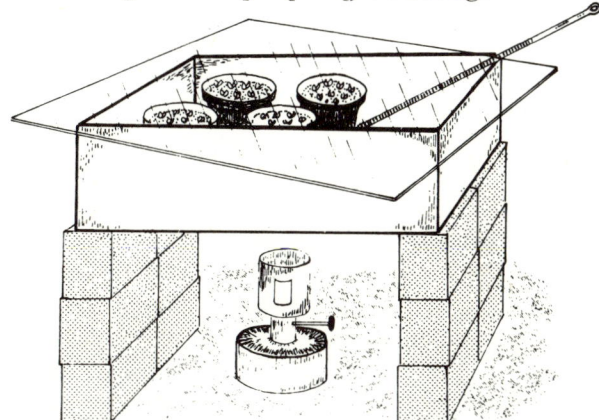

Fig. 17. An improvised propagating or seed-raising box. A layer of moist sand on the bottom distributes heat evenly and maintains humidity. An electric heater or electric bulb can be substituted for the oil lamp.

Plate 33. An electrically heated garden frame can be used for seed raising and propagating without a greenhouse.

Where a reasonable amount of space is available, an excellent seed germinator and propagating case can be made using a heating cable (Plate 33). Heating cables are usually designed to operate on low voltage supplied by a transformer that renders them extremely safe. For outdoor use in the open garden soil, the low-voltage type is definitely preferable because of possible accidental damage to the cable from garden tools.

To construct a cable-warmed propagator all that is needed is a stout wooden tray of well-seasoned warp-resistant wood, or a deep galvanized tray such as is used on greenhouse benches. In this is placed a layer of fine sand in which the heating cable is embedded. The cable should be so arranged as to give at least 15 watts to the square foot and should preferably be in circuit with a rod-type thermostat. If a thermostat cannot be used, the wattage per square foot should be reduced to prevent possible overheating. About 11 watts can be tried. The cable should be immersed in the sand so that it is at least half an inch from the bottom of the tray and is covered by at least 2 inches of sand. Tents of glass can then be placed on the top to keep in the warmth and moisture

Growing Plants from Seed 115

without risk of the glass cutting into the cable. Ideally, of course, properly framed glass should be used to cover the warming bench (Fig. 18).

An outdoor garden frame can be similarly fitted with a heating cable, and there are specially designed frames available already fitted with cables and thermostat (Plate 33).

The sand must always be kept moist, because moist sand conducts the heat from the cable better as well as providing atmospheric moisture in the case or frame. An outdoor frame can have the glass lined with plastic sheeting during winter to conserve warmth and save fuel.

It has been a common practice to cover the cable-warmed sand with peat in which the containers of seeds or pots of plants were buried. I find that for most work involving germination and the early care of seedlings that practice is un-

Plate 34. A propagating and seed-raising bench warmed by an electric cable. To attain different temperatures according to requirements, some of the pans are covered with glass "tents."

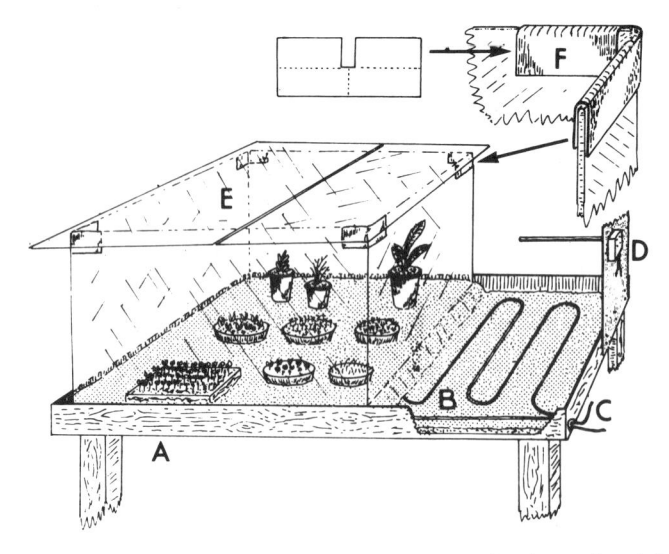

Fig. 18. A homemade propagating case: (A) wooden tray about 6 inches deep; (B) soil-warming cable on a layer of sand; (C) cable wired to be controlled by the thermostat (D) if desired; (E) sheets of glass held together by the arrangement of bent sheet metal (F). The metal is cut in the pattern illustrated and bent along the dotted lines.

necessary provided that the warming bed is equipped with a frame of some kind. The peat can be more nuisance than it is worth, and there seems to be no necessity to bury the seed pans or pots since the atmosphere in a closed case reaches a temperature approaching that of the warmed sand flooring. Pricked-out seedlings of many bedding and decorative pot plants can, however, be buried in peat with advantage when they are being raised in quantity in a greenhouse with a minimum temperature of about 45° F. This matter is further discussed under the heading "After-care of Seedlings," page 120.

A similar seed-raising case based on a tray of moist sand can be warmed by an oil heater or properly designed greenhouse electric heater, such as the tubular type. Where hot-water pipes are fitted in a greenhouse the seed raiser can be constructed over them at a suitable distance to provide the required interior temperature. Electric fan heaters are not

Growing Plants from Seed 117

really suitable, and the ordinary domestic electric coil of the glowing element should never be used. The latter can be dangerous in damp places like a greenhouse where water is likely to be sprayed about.

It should be remembered that the temperature attained by a propagating case—if it is not thermostatically controlled—is dependent on the temperature of the surroundings. On a warm day the temperature may rise too high, and during a cold night it may fall to much lower than is desirable. Using electric heating with a thermostatic control avoids such fluctuations and the necessity for constant attention.

Most commercial electric propagators (Plate 35) are well designed, and the temperature attained can be predetermined by means of a calibrated dial. Some do suffer from the disadvantage that they will not reach a sufficiently high temperature for the germination of seeds of certain tropical plants, such as palms. The purchaser should therefore be sure that the propagator will suit the work for which it is re-

Plate 35. A thermostatically controlled electric propagator.

quired. Sometimes the manufacturer can fix extra heating elements, which enable higher temperatures to be reached. A useful propagator suitable for raising many unusual and tropical subjects should reach about 80° F.

Containers for Germination

Containers for seed mixes in which the seeds are germinated can consist of small pots for large seeds, clay seed pans, or seed trays that can be made from a variety of materials such as wood and plastic. The size of the container should of course be chosen to suit the number of seeds being sown—but whatever type of container is used must be absolutely clean. To use dirty old seed boxes that have been left around the garden is asking for failure. Nowadays wooden boxes can be avoided anyway. Excellent plastic types are available that do not rot and are easily cleaned and sterilized in a few minutes. Plastic pots are also superior for many purposes and save a great deal of work because they are so easily cleaned. Plants in plastic pots need less watering, which is an additional great advantage, and after personal experience in growing a very wide range of common and uncommon plants in such pots I can recommend them with confidence.

Sowing the Seed

Seed should always be sown sparingly so as to leave ample room for pricking out. Often sowings can be made in spring to give benefit the same year and in autumn to give results the following year. It is a great mistake to raise so many seedlings that they cause overcrowding and cannot be accommodated or looked after properly.

Shallow sowings are to be preferred, and it should be remembered not to cover seeds requiring light for germination. The soil mix must be well moistened prior to sowing, and if clay pans are used these should have been thoroughly soaked by immersion in water for several hours.

After sowing, the treatment of the seeds will vary depending on their nature. It will usually be an advantage to

Growing Plants from Seed   119

cover the containers with sheets of glass which keep in the moisture. But when a propagator covered with a frame or some other glass enclosure is used, it may be better to leave the pans uncovered unless there is excessive condensate drip from the roof of the case.

Covering the containers with paper should not be a standard procedure, as is often indiscriminately recommended. We have already seen that some types of seed will not germinate well, if at all, unless exposed to light. When in doubt it is best to surface sow some of the seeds and to cover others with soil and leave the container uncovered with paper where it can receive maximum daylight. Any difference in germination can be noted for future guidance.

The advantage of covering the seed pans with paper is that the darkened soil mix is unable to grow algae, which can interfere with aeration. Should the seeds take a long time to germinate, such algal growth can be a nuisance. It is also better, if paper is used, to employ absorbent paper and to place it under the glass. The condensate of water which invariably forms on the underside of the glass is then prevented from dripping onto the seeds and inducing a soggy surface condition. (Fig 19).

It is essential that as soon as germination takes place any covering excluding light from the pan is immediately removed, or the seedlings will become drawn and useless. An inspection for germination should be made every morning.

Any watering that may be necessary after sowing to keep

Fig. 19. A prepared seed pan. (Note that the glass is over the top of the paper, but it is not always advisable to exclude light.)

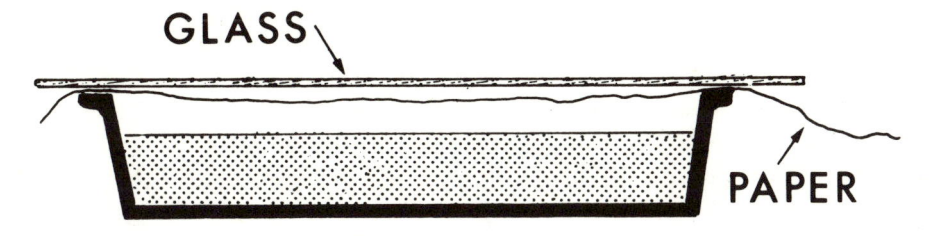

GLASS

PAPER

the soil moist during germination should be done with a sprayer delivering a fine spray or mist of water, which will penetrate very efficiently without disturbing the seeds. This is especially important in the case of surface-sown seeds.

After-care of Seedlings

It is of no use taking great care to achieve success in germinating seeds if the resulting seedlings are spoiled by lack of attention to simple requirements. Because a seed needs a high temperature for germination, it does not follow that the plant will also require considerable warmth, and gardeners should not be discouraged. For example, many popular house plants will survive very low temperatures during winter although they are of tropical origin. Sometimes they may shed a few leaves in protest—Begonia rex often does this—but when the temperature rises in spring they quickly regain their attractive appearance. The important proviso is that any change in a plant's growing conditions must be made gradually. With regard to temperature change, hardening-off is commonly enough practiced, but similar conditioning must also be given when changes in light intensity are concerned. For example, many decorative conservatory or house plants will grow well in the shade, or even in gloom, and equally well in bright light—provided that the change from one to the other is made gradually over a period of time. The most disastrous change is from shade to full sunlight, when the plants are often seriously scorched. Even the notoriously hardy aspidistra will not put up with this.

Immediately after germination seedlings need as much light as possible—but not full sunlight if they are being raised under glass, unless they are well known to be sun lovers.

If despite the use of proper soils the seedlings are seen to become weak and spindly, the temperature may be too high or the light insufficient. If little growth is made, the temperature is probably too low, but seedlings of some plants—e.g., streptocarpus—naturally develop very slowly at first.

A good, healthy root system is essential to all plants, and

for vigorous root formation seedlings require a reasonable root temperature. It is often an advantage if the pots or boxes can be buried in peat on a warming bench, and when this is done it is desirable for the air temperature to be lower than that of the peat so that top growth is not forced. In a cool greenhouse with a minimum air temperature of about 45° F., a covering for the warming bench may be unnecessary, depending on the type of plants grown. It is certainly not required for ordinary half-hardy bedding plants. Tropical and subtropical plants may be less happy with these conditions and usually make much more initial growth if kept in a covered propagator. For this reason a propagator with plenty of height to allow plant growth to an advanced stage is often desirable.

Soil Mixes and Fertilizers for Seedlings and Potted Plants

The ideal situation for the private individual is to have his own privately controlled source of composted soil available. Commercially supplied soil stripped from farm fields generally is dangerously high in excess soluble salts and/or worse yet contains residues of weed killers that are deadly for almost all ornamentals.

Reliable commercially packaged soil mixes are available in department store garden departments, garden centers, hardware stores, and variety stores. Special mixes can be obtained for the most commonly grown house plants. Many of these mixes contain no natural soil but are soilless mixtures of peat and perlite or peat and vermiculite. The better ones even contain the proper amount of slow-release fertilizers. Even some professional producers of millions of plants for sale buy the soil mixes they use from soil-mixing specialists because the soil is reliable and cheaper in the long run.

Because of the high proportion of peat in most of these mixes it is essential to moisten them very thoroughly before use, as it is very difficult to do so after they are in the plant container. Fortunately, with no clay particles in the mix there is no danger of overpacking the soil by handling it while it is wet. The great porosity of these mixes permits rapid runthrough of water and prevents dangerous salt buildup, but it also makes more frequent fertilizing necessary. Soluble fertilizers are best for this purpose. Many commercial growers use injectors in their water lines that pick up a slight amount of fertilizer solution every time the plants are watered. This system, termed "constant feed," is the ideal way to grow plants.

This system is generally not very practical for most laymen although it is not impossible. A stronger solution used less frequently is more practical. It is better to mix the solution fresh each time it is used to avoid chemical reaction between the ingredients themselves or in combination with the salts already present in the water. There are a number of brands of soluble fertilizers on the market.

More easily used by the layman are the various fertilizer tablets on the market. Some are placed right in the soil while planting large outdoor plants or indoor plants and are long lasting with slow release. Claims are made that some of them feed up to three years. Another type, which is placed on top of the container, disintegrates and enters the soil with subsequent waterings. Still others are inserted in the soil periodically as shown on the directions for the kind and size of plant.

There is one advantage to heavier soils than those recommended above, if reliable loam is available. In the case of container-grown plants, especially woody ones that are expected to remain in the same container for several years, the heavier soil does not "wear out" as rapidly. It retains plant food better and, being low in organic matter, does not shrink.

On the other hand, seedling mixes should be even lighter and more porous than potting soils. The accepted practice for sowing seed now is to spread over the light porous soil a thin layer of horticultural-grade milled sphagnum moss to sow the seed in. Sphagnum is inherently antibiotic and prevents

Growing Plants from Seed   123

"damping off." It is also easy to transplant from the sphagnum without damaging the roots of the seedlings.

Germinating Fern Spores

A number of seed dealers are now supplying the spores of uncommon ferns, including Staghorn fern (page 97), but the germination technique is not generally known.

Ferns do not flower; they form a botanical class quite apart from the more familiar flowering plants. In prehistoric times conditions were very different, and they were widespread. Their prolific growth has resulted in much of our coal, in which their fossilized fronds can often be seen as a reminder of their majestic past.

Ferns reproduce by means of spores that in most cases are formed directly on the undersides of the fronds. The

Plate 36. Prothalli, the first stage in the growth of ferns, are formed before true germination takes place.

124 GROWING EXOTIC PLANTS INDOORS

Plate 37. A prothallus greatly enlarged, showing the true fern leaf just forming after germination has taken place.

spores are minute and have the appearance of fine brown dust, and their germination process is entirely different from the comparative one of ordinary seeds. Fertilization occurs after "germination," and to enable this to take place the first step is the formation of a structure called a prothallus (Plate 36), which contains both male and female organs. The prothalli are very small, translucent, pale green, and heart-shaped. Nothing could look less like fern growth, and the inexperienced have sometimes thrown away the first stage in the growth of their ferns thinking the prothalli to be some undesirable lichen.

To allow fertilization of the egg cell by a sperm it is necessary for a film of water to cover the surface of the prothallus, and it is consequently important that the atmosphere above the prothalli should be kept moist when they have formed. After fertilization a tiny typical fern frond begins to develop and form its own roots (Plate 37); the pro-

Growing Plants from Seed 125

thallus, having served its purpose, then withers.

This may sound complicated, but the practical details are quite simple. The spores should be sparingly sprinkled on the surface of a mixture consisting of equal parts of sterilized loam, silica sand, fine peat, and fine sterilized leaf mold. (Leaf mold may be sterilized by pouring boiling water on to it and allowing it to drain.) The mixture should be contained in a pot or pan with drainage holes covered with a thick layer of coarse grit or crushed pumice. The pot is stood in an inch or so of water so that the water may rise by capillary action, thus maintaining very moist conditions. To keep the air over the spores humid, the pots or pans must be covered with glass, which must be left in position until the first signs of the formation of true fern fronds, which indicates that fertilization has taken place. In the meantime the pots should have

Plate 38. Arrangement for germinating fern spores. The pots are placed in a tray of water and covered with glass to keep a high humidity until the first true fern leaves are formed.

been kept in a shady place and the water in which they are standing added to as necessary (Plate 38). The temperature required depends on the type of ferns being raised. Most greenhouse ferns need about 70° F. for development of the prothallus, but the hardy kinds will be happy with very much lower temperatures.

A very approximate time for the appearance of prothalli is about 2-4 weeks. A further period of about 8 weeks may elapse before the true fronds begin to develop. Most ferns prefer an acid soil with a pH of about 6.0 and partial shade. The best time for sowing the spores is in early spring.

It is usually impracticable to prick out the prothalli with the developing fronds individually, so they are what is known as "patched out." This entails pricking out a small group, ensuring that a portion with a developing frond is selected. The pricking out can be made into seed boxes or pots of a similar soil mix. Sometimes a light peat and leaf mold mix will be found to suit ferns quite well.

Cultural Troubles with Uncommon Plants

It may sometimes be difficult to discover why a plant is not growing satisfactorily if details of its cultivation are not readily available, but nearly all plants react similarly if they are not pleased with the main essentials of their treatment—temperature, watering, soil conditions, and light.

Slow growth can be caused by low temperature or by a poor or unsatisfactory soil. It can also be caused by excessive watering, which may have started root rot. Overwatering is the cause of many plant casualties, and when in doubt it is safer to underwater. It is much easier to revive an underwatered plant than to save an overwatered specimen with rotted roots. Common symptoms of overwatering are leaf yellowing, leaf fall, and the dropping of flowers and buds.

The shedding of leaves is usually the sign of protest in tropical subjects that are not receiving enough warmth or have not been conditioned to lower temperatures over a long enough period, and bleaching of leaf color and markings in shade lovers exposed to too much light. Insufficient light is usually indicated by lanky growth and the development of yellowing due to the lack of chlorophyll formation. Yellowing of the foliage can also be caused if the soil pH is not suitable. Perhaps lime should be omitted from the soil, or the water may be too hard.

Pests and diseases can simulate these symptoms, and regular inspection of the under surfaces of leaves should be made as a routine measure. That is where many plant pests first make their appearance.

SUPPLIERS OF UNUSUAL AND EXOTIC PLANTS

Alpenglow Gardens
13328 Trans-Canda Highway
Surray PO, B.C., Canada

Arthur Eames Allgrove
281 Woburn St.
No. Wilmington, MA 01887

The Bamboo Man
Box 331
Saddle River, NJ

Blackthorne Gardens
48 Quincy St.
Holbrook, MA 02343
(R.W. Bemis)

Bolduc's Green Hills Nursery
2131 Vallejo St.
St. Helena, CA 94571

California Jungle Gardens
11977 San Vicente Blvd.
Los Angeles, CA 90049

Central Nursery Co.
2675 Johnson Ave.
San Luis Obispo, CA 93401

The Garden Spot
4032 Rosewood Dr.
Columbia, SC 29205
(W.G. Freeland)

International Growers'
Exchange, Inc.
P.O. Box 397
Farmington, MI 48024

J.L. Hudson, Seedsman
P.O. Box 1058
Redwood City, CA 94064

Ken Foster
3822 Larkston Dr.
Orange, CA 92667

Logee's Greenhouse
55 North St.
Danielson, CT 06239

Martin Viette Nurseries
Northern Blvd.
East Norwich, LI, NY 11732

Mellinger's, Inc.
2310 W. South Range Rd.
North Lima, OH 44452

Merry Gardens
P.O. Box 68
Camden, ME 04843

New Mexico Cactus Research
P.O. Box 787
Belen, NM 87002

Nichol's Garden Nursery
1190 N. Pacific Hghwy.
Albany, OR 97321

Park Gardens
1435 Huntington Tnpke.
Trumbull, CT 06611

Select Nurseries, Inc.
12831 E. Central Ave.
Brea, CA

Sharon Nursery
P.O. Box 1172
925 N.W. 10th Ave.
Boynton Beach, FL 33435

Springbrook Gardens
6776 Husley Rd.
Mentor, OH 44060

The Tool Shed Herb Nursery
Turkey Hill Rd.
Purdy Station
Salem Center, NY 10578

Vaughan's Seed Store
533 Katrine Ave.
Downers Grove, IL 60515

W.J. Brudy
113 Aucila Rd.
Box 84
Cocoa Beach, FL 32931

GENERAL INDEX

A

Abyssinian banana tree, 96-97, illus. 95
Acacia, 22, 35-36
Acclimatization of plants, 105-6
African violet, 8-9, 10, illus. 8
Air layering, 74
Air rooting, 73-74
Amur maple tree, 42
Aquatic plants, 48
Araceae family, 99-100
Aristolochias, 79-82, illus. 81
Artillery plant, 49
Art pot, 3
Asparagus fern, 22, 35
Australian pitcher plant, 63-64, illus. 63
Austrian pine, 42
Automatic watering systems, 9-10 illus. 10
Auxin, 48

B

Banana tree, 94-97
Banyan tree, 36
Barberry tree, 42
Bay windows, 17, illus. 17
Begonias, 109
  rex, 3, 8, 106, 120
Bessemer conservatory, 18
Bindweed, 85
Bird of paradise flower, 100-103, illus. 101
Bird's nest spruce, 42
Black hill spruce, 42
Bladder senna, 89
Bladderwort, 69-70, illus. 70
Bleaching powder, 111-12

Bonsai, 39-46, illus. 38, 41, 43, 46
  containers, 44
  displaying, 45-46
  plants suitable for, 42
  training, 43-44
Bottle gardens, 28-35, illus. 29, 30, 32
  plants suitable for, 34-35
  soil, 29, 31
British butterwort, 68
Bromeliads, 34-35, 82-85, illus. 82
  flowering of, 85
Bromelian, 60, 83
Butterwort, 68

C

Cabbage palm, 25-26
Cacti and succulents, 3, 29, 92
Calcium hypochlorite, 111-12
Carnivorous plants, 57-77, illus. 59
  culture, 61-62
  feeding, 76-77
Castor oil plant, 35
Cephalotaceae family, 63-64
Chameleon plant, 85
Charcoal, as soil additive, 31
Cinerarias, 109
Clay pots, 4
Climbing plants, 18
Coconut palm, 24, 28, illus. 24
Coffee plants, 36
Coleus, 109
Column limber pine, 42
Conservatories, 15-22, illus. 19, 20
  construction of, 18-21
  palm care, 26-28

General Index 131

Containers, 3-4. See also Plant Cases; Planters; Terrariums
 bonsai, 44
 seed sowing, 118
Convolvulus family, 85-87, 94
Cotton wool pads, for germination, 111
Crimson pygmy barberry, 42
Crocuses, 48
Cultivation of plants, 105-27
Curly palm, 25

D

Darlingtonia family, 74-75, 106, illus. 75
Date palm, 25
Dehydration of plant cells, 49
Diseases, plant, 32-33, 127
Doum palm, 23
Drainage, 4, 5
Droseras, 60, 64-67, illus. 59, 65
Dutchman's pipe, illus. 81
Dwarf Alberta Spruce, 42
Dwarf conifers, 22, 41-42
Dwarf date palm, 25
Dwarf fern, 34
Dwarf trees, 39-46, illus. 38, 41 43, 46

E

Enzymes, plant, 60-61, 74, 76
Epiphytic plants, 4, 83, 98
Everlasting flowers, 22

F

Fan-leaved palm, 26
Fan palm, 26
Ferns, 3, 8, 11, 14, 37. See also names of ferns as Asparagus fern; Staghorn fern
 propagation, 123-26
Ferrous sulphate, 28
Fertilizers, 6, 28, 59-60, 71, 122
Fiberglass, 4, 20-21
Ficin, 61
Fig tree, 61

Fittonias, 14, 34
Flagella, 48
Flat palm, 25
Flowering house plants, 9, 14-15, 84
Flowering quince, 42
Fluorescent lighting, 6-9, illus. 8
Formic acid, 76

G

Gas burners, effect on plants, 3
Geotropism, 48
Germination of seeds. See Seeds, subhead Germination
Gibberellic acid, 109
Glass substitutes, 14, 21
Glory pea, 87-90, illus. 87
Gomuti palm, 23
Grafting seedlings, 89-90
Gravitation, effect on plants, 48
Gray mold, 33
Greenhouses, 15-17, 22
 construction of, 13-14, illus. 11
Green vitriol, 28

H

Heliamphora, 75
Histamine, 61
Humidity, 6

I

Incubators, seed, 112-18, illus. 113, 114, 116, 117, 119
Indian lotus, 107
Indoor gardens. See Conservatories; Greenhouses; Plant cases; Terrariums
Insect control. See Diseases, Plant
Insectivorous plants, 57-58, 59, 75 illus. 59, 68, 75
Iron sulfate, 28
Ivy, 2

J

Japanese black pine, 42

132 General Index

Japanese bonsai, 39, 40-41
Japanese fern balls, 90-92, illus. 91
Japanese juniper, 42
Japanese white pine, 42
Jumping beans, 49-50

K

Kentias, 25

L

Leaf mold, 125
Leguminosae family, 49, 53-55, 87-90
Lentibulariaceae family, 68-70
Light
 artificial, 6-9, illus. 8
 effect of, on plants, 3, 6, 48-49
 effect of, on seeds, 109
Lithops, 92
Living stones, 92
Lobster claw, 87-88
Loquat, bonsai, illus. 43

M

Maidenhair tree, 42
Malus, 42
Maple trees, grown as bonsai, 42
Marantas, 3, 8, 15, 34
Medicinal plants, 80
Mescal button, 92-94, illus. 93
Mescalin, effects of, 93-94
Mimosa, 52
Miniature roses, 22
Moisture control, 6
Monarch of the East, 99-100, illus. 100
Moonflower, 85-87, illus. 86
Morning glory, 85, 86, 94
Motile plants, 47-55
Movement in plants, 47-55
Mugho pine, 42
Musaceae family, 94-97

N

Natural habitat of plants, 105-6

Nepenthaceae family, 60, 70-74
New Zealand lobster claw, 87-88
Nikau palm, 26
North exposure, 3

O

Oil Palm, 25
Orchids, 14, 112, illus. 12
Ornamental pepper, illus. 104
Oxalidaceae family, 49, 55-56

P

Palms, 3, 22-28, 106, 109 See also names of palms, as Date palm
 culture, 26-28
Papain, 60
Papaw, 61
Parrot's bill, 87-88
Pea family, 49
Peat moss, 4-5, 115-16
Peperomia, 3, 8, 14, 34
Pepper, ornamental, illus. 104
Pests. See Diseases, plant
Philodendron, 3, 37
Phototropism, 48
Pineapple family, 60, 82-85, illus. 82
Pine trees, 42
Pitcher plant, Australian, 63-64
Pitcher plants, 58, 60, 61, 70-76, 77-78, illus. 75
Plant cases, 11-15, 22
 construction of, 13-14, illus. 13
Planters, 9-10, illus. 10. See also Containers
Plant food. See Fertilizers
Plant movement, 47-55
Plant windows, 15-17, illus. 16-17
Plastic, as substitute for glass, 14
Plastic bags to keep plants moist, 2
Plastic containers, 4, 118
Plastic insulation, 17, 115
Potsherds, 5
Pots. See Containers
Pots within pots, 3

General Index   133

Potting, 5-6
Potting soil. See Soil
Propagation. See also Seeds
　air rooting, 73-74
　air layering, 74
　fern spores, 123-26
Propagators, seed, 112-18, illus.
　113, 114, 116, 117, 119
Proteolytic enzymes, 60-61, 74, 76,
　83
Prothalli, 124, 126, illus. 123,
　124
Pulvini, 49

Q

Quartz glass, 21
Quince, flowering, 42

R

Rain water, 62
Rex begonia, 3, 8, 106, 120
Root pruning, 44-45
Root rot, 126
Roses, miniature, 22
Round-leaved sundew, 64
Rubber plant, 36

S

Saghalin spruce, 42
Salt encrustation, on pots, 6
Sarraceniaceae family, 74-76, 106,
　illus. 75
Scarifying process, 110
Scotch pine, 42
Seedlings, 120-23
Seed pods, 49
Seeds, 35-37, 52
　containers, 118
　germination, 108-10
　incubators, 112-18, illus. 113,
　　114, 116, 117, 119
　soaking, 110
　soil, 110-11
　sowing, 118-19
　storage, 108
　viability of, 107-8

Semaphore plant. See Telegraph
　plant
Sensitive plant, 47, 50-52, illus. 50,
　51
Shade plants, 3, 8
Silver thatch palm, 26
Sleep movement, 49, 55
Soil, 121-23
　seed germination, 110-11
　temperature, 4
　terrarium, 29, 31
Soil-less seed germination, 111-12
Solar gray glass, 21
Sphagnum moss, 62, 71, 123
Spruce trees, 42
Staghorn fern, 97-99, illus. 78
Succulents, 3, 92
Sun porches, 18-22, illus. 20
　palm care, 26-28
　plants suitable for, 22, 35, 36
Sweet pea, 110

T

Telegraph plant, 47, 49, 53-55,
　illus. 53
Temperature control, 2, 11, 14, 48
　soil, 4
　terrariums, 33
Terrariums, 28-35, illus. 12, 13,
　29, 30, 32
　plants for, 34-35
　soil, 29, 31
Thermostat, 14
Thiourea treatment, 109
Tiddly winks, 37
Touch sensitive plants, 50-56
Trees, dwarf, 39-46, illus. 38, 41,
　43, 46
Trident maple tree, 42
Trumpet leaf, 75
Tulips, 48
Turgor action, 49, 58

V

Venus's flytrap, 47, 60, 66-67, 76,
　illus. 66

General Index

W

Wardian cases, 11
Watering, 2, 4, 5, 62, 83, 126
Water plants, 48
Western silver wattle, 35
Window boxes, 4

Wintergreen boxwood, 42
Wistaria, 42

Z

Zebrina, 3, 29
Zelkovia elm, *illus.* 38

BOTANICAL INDEX

A

Acacia baileyana, 35
—— *brachybotrya*, 35
—— *dealbata*, 35, 52
—— *decora*, 35
—— *discolor*, 35
Acer buergerianum, 42
—— *ginnala*, 42
Aechmea rhodocyanea, 84
Amorphophallus giganteus, 99
Ananas comosus, 82
Anthurium, 14
Aralia elegantissima, 106
—— *sieboldii*, 35
Araucaria excelsa, 3
Archontophoenix cunninghamiana, 26, illus. 27
Areca catechu, 23
—— *sapida*, 26
Aregelia carolinae, 34, illus. 82
Arenga saccharifera, 23
Aristolochia elegans, 57-58, 80-82, 106, illus. 81
—— *indica*, 80
—— *reticulata*, 80
Arum cornutum, 99
Asparagus plumosus nana, 35
—— *sprengeri*, 35
Aspidistra, 2

B

Baphia nitida, 15
Begonia rex, 3, 8, 106, 120
Berberis thunbergii atropurpurea nana, 42
Bertolonia marmorata, 15, 106
Bilbergia nutans, 84
Biophytum sensitivum, 14, 55-56, illus. 57

Bougainvillea, 18
Butia capitata, 25
—— *yatay*, 25
Buxus koreana microphylla, 42

C

Calamus draco, 23
Calathea lubbersiana, 34
Calonyction aculeatum, 85-87
Cannabis indica, 22
Carica papaya, 61, 106
Carissa grandiflora nana, 42
Caryota urens, 23
Cephalotus follicularis, 63-64, illus. 63
Chaenomeles, 42
Chamaedorea elegans, 26
Chamaerops excelsa, 26, illus. 27
—— *humilis*, 26
Chlorophytum, 3
Citrus mitis, 22
Clianthus formosus, 88-90, illus. 89
—— *puniceus*, 87-88
Cocos australis, 25
—— *nucifera*, 24, illus. 24
—— *weddelliana*, 25
—— *yatay*, 25
Coffea arabica, 36, 106
Colchicum, 22
Coleus, 109
Colutea arborescens, 89-90, illus. 89
Convolvulus arrensis, 85
Copernica cerifera, 23
Cordyline indivisa, 36
Crassula arborescens, 42
Crocus sativus, 22
Cryptanthus aculis rubra, 34

Botanical Index

—— bivittatus, 34, 85, illus. 82
—— zonatus, 85

D

Daemonorops draco, 23
Darlingtonia californica, 75, illus. 75
Davallia mariesii, 34, 90-92, illus. 91
Desmodium gyrans, 49, 53-55, illus. 53
Dionaea muscipula, 15, 66-67, illus. 66
Dracaena indivisa, 22, 36
Drosera angelica, 64
—— binata, 64, 65, illus. 65
—— capensis, 64
—— longifolia, 64
—— rotundifolia, 64
—— spathulata, 64
Drosophyllum lusitanicum, 22, 67

E

Elaeis guineensis, 25
Eucalyptus globulus, 22, 36
Exacum affine, 37

F

Fatshedera, 3
Fatsia japonica, 3, 22, 35
Ficus benghalensis, 22, 36
—— carica, 61
—— elastica, 36, 106
Fittonia argyroneura, 34
Fuchsia, 106

G

Gentianacae, 37
Ginkgo biloba, 42, illus. 41
Grevillea robusta, 22, 36-37

H

Hedera canariensis, 2
Heliamphora nutans, 75

Helxine, 29
Hevea brasiliensis, 36
Holmstrup arborvitae, 42
Howea belmoreana, 25
—— forsteriana, 25
Hyphaene thebaica, 23

I

Impatiens, 109
Isolepis gracilis, 106

J

Jacaranda mimosaefolia, 22, 36-37
Juniperus chinensis, 42
—— procumbens, 42

L

Lithops, 92
Livistona chinensis, 26
Lobelia tenuior, 15
Lodoicea sechellarum, 24
Lophophora williamsii, 22, 92-94

M

Mallotus philippinensis, 15
Maranta leuconeura, 34
—— —— massangeana, 34
Metroxylon laeve, 23
—— rumphii, 23
Mimosa pudica, 15, 22, 50-52, 56, illus 50, 51
—— sensitiva, 50, 56
Moluccella laevis, 106
Morongia uncinata, 56
Musa ensete, 22, 96-97, illus 95

N

Neanthe elegans, 26
Nelumbo nucifera, 107
Neoregelia carolinae tricolor, 85
Nepenthes gracilis, 72
—— hookeriana, 71
—— khasiana, 70, 72-73, illus. 72, 73
—— rafflesiana, 71, 72

Botanical Index

Neptunia oleraceae, 55, illus. 56
Nipa fruticans, 24

O

Oreodoxa oleracea, 25-26
—— regia, 26
—— sancona, 25
Oxalis sensitiva, 55-56

P

Pelargonium, 22
Pellaea cordata, 37
Pellionia daveauana, 34
Peperomia caperata, 34
—— galloides, 34
—— hederafolia, 34
—— rubella, 34
Pharbitis tricolor, 85
Philodendron bipinnatifidum, 37
Phoenix dactylifera, 25
—— roebelinii, 25
Phytelephas macrocarpa, 23
Picea abies nidiformis, 42
—— glauca conica, 42
—— glauca densata, 42
—— glehni, 42
Pilea cadierei, 15, 34
—— muscosa, 49
Pinguicula bakeriana, 68-69, illus. 68
—— caudata, 68-69
—— grandiflora, 68
—— vulgaris, 68
Pinus flexilis columnaris, 42
—— mugho mughus, 42
—— nigra, 42
—— parviflora pentaphylla, 42
—— sylvestris, 42
—— thunbergii, 42
Piper ornatum, illus. 104
Platycerium alcicorne, 98
—— bifurcatum, 97-99

Punica granatum, 22

R

Raphia, 23
Rhapalostylis sapida, 26
Ricinus communis, 22

S

Saintpaulia ionantha, 8-9, 10, 15, 34, illus. 8
Sansevieria, 29
Sauromatum guttatum, 22, 99-100, illus. 100
Schefflera digitata, 37
Scirpus cernuus, 106
Seaforthia elegans, 26, illus. 27
Selaginella, 15, 34
Stenocarpus sinuatus, 3
Stillingia palmeri, 50
Strelitzia regina, 100-103, 106, illus. 101
Syagrus weddelliana, 25

T

Tetranema mexicanum, 14, 35
Thrinax argenta, 26
Thuja occidentalis holmstrup, 42
Trachycarpus fortunei, 26, illus. 27

U

Utricularia vulgaris, 69-70, illus. 70

V

Vriesia splendens, 35, 85, illus. 82

Z

Zebrina pendula, 3